Africa in the Indian Imagination

AFRICA IN THE
INDIAN IMAGINATION
Race and the Politics of Postcolonial Citation

Antoinette Burton

Duke University Press   Durham and London

Foreword by Isabel Hofmeyr © 2016 Duke University Press.
Originally published as *Brown over Black: Race and the Politics of Postcolonial Citation* by Three Essays Collective, India.
© Three Essays 2012.
All rights reserved.

Library of Congress Cataloging-in-Publication Data
Names: Burton, Antoinette M., [date] author. | Hofmeyr, Isabel, writer of foreword.
Title: Africa in the Indian imagination : race and the politics of postcolonial citation / Antoinette Burton ; foreword by Isabel Hofmeyr
Other titles: Brown over black
Description: Durham : Duke University Press, 2016. | Includes bibliographical references and index. | Originally published as Brown over Black by Gurgaon : Three Essays Collective, 2012.
Identifiers: LCCN 2015042544
ISBN 9780822361480 (hardcover)
ISBN 9780822361671 (pbk.)
ISBN 9780822374138 (e-book)
Subjects: LCSH: India—Relations—Africa. | Africa—Relations—India. | Race—Political aspects—India. | Race—Political aspects—Africa. | Postcolonialism—India. | Postcolonialism—Africa. | Indic fiction (English)—20th century—History and criticism. | Race in literature.
Classification: LCC DS450.A35 B87 2016 | DDC 303.48/25406—dc23
LC record available at http://lccn.loc.gov/2015042544

Cover art: Sam Machia, ink on paper. Illustration by Sam Machia.

For Phyllis Naidoo and Stuart Hall, Stuart Hall and Phyllis Naidoo
equally, differently, jointly

with appreciation for all I have learned from them
about politics, struggle, courage and heart

Exploitation and domination of one nation over another can have no place in a world striving to put an end to all wars.

Mohandas K. Gandhi, Bombay 1945

Contents

Foreword by Isabel Hofmeyr   ix
Acknowledgments   xiii

Introduction
Citing/Siting Africa in the Indian Postcolonial Imagination   1

Chapter 1
"Every Secret Thing"? Racial Politics in Ansuyah R. Singh's
    Behold the Earth Mourns (1960)   27

Chapter 2
Race and the Politics of Position: Above and Below in Frank
    Moraes' *The Importance of Being Black* (1965)   57

Chapter 3
Fictions of Postcolonial Development:
    Race, Intimacy and Afro-Asian Solidarity in Chanakya Sen's
    The Morning After (1973)   89

Chapter 4
Hands and Feet: Phyllis Naidoo's Impressions of
    Anti-apartheid History (2002–2006)   123

Epilogue   167

Index   173

Foreword
Isabel Hofmeyr

In its form, content, and making, this book is a portable experiment. Each essay is devoted to one novel or work of nonfiction and the volume convenes a speculative bookshelf comprising texts whose authors and characters rove widely—from Bombay to Durban; Goa to Ghana; Uganda to India. These itineraries crisscross previously colonized parts of the world creating a constellation of pathways in what we now call the global south, itself an experimental configuration whose outline and import are currently far from clear.

As the significance of the global south as a geopolitical force gains momentum, opinion on what it is or how it might be understood proliferate. Is it the post-American future toward which the debt-stricken West is inevitably evolving? Could it be the portent of what a sustainable future might look like? Or, is it in fact the future of capitalism itself, as postcolonial elites entrench themselves through enabling devastating forms of extractive labor while creating new multilateral power alignments like BRICS? Or, is this multilateralism in fact an anti- or perhaps semi-capitalist arrangement that could shift the gravity of world power southward? Others insist on the global south as the post-89 instantiation of the "third world," where older traditions of anti-imperialism will be reprised in the new neoliberal order, making the global south the locus of radical global social movements. An aesthetic variation on this theme portrays the global south as the space of creativity in, despite, and at times because of chaos, uncertainty, and volatility—the global south as artistic credo. A more melancholic version of this orientation characterizes the global south as the graveyard of grand schemes in which the ruins and remainders of master narratives—imperialism, anti-colonialism, socialism, apartheid, anti-apartheid—pile up, creating ideological rubbish dumps in which people must make their lives.

To make sense of the global south, we need modes of enquiry that encompass all these possibilities. There are a number of contemporary studies that attempt such a task. Ching Kwan Lee has undertaken detailed ethnographic work on Chinese investment enclaves in Zambia and Tanzania. Her pathbreaking work illustrates the divergent outcomes in both places and the differing sets of worker responses to the casualization of labor. Lee's work dismantles alarmist aggregate statistics about supposed Chinese neo-imperialism in Africa even as she demonstrates a painful story of "African socialism [meets] structural adjustment [meets] Chinese investment." As she notes, "Neither Chinese capital nor Africa is singular, and the dynamic of their encounters, raw in many ways . . . can be grasped only from within and across these Chinese enclaves."[1]

Africa in the Indian Imagination enters a cognate domain of complexity: the historical archive of interactions between "Africa" and "India." The lattice of linkages between these two regions is old and deep—ancient monsoon-driven trade routes across the Indian Ocean; massive imperial flows of labor between the two regions; relationships of anti-colonial and anti-apartheid support and solidarity; and more recently a neoliberal wave of Indian investment in the continent.

These exchanges and interactions constitute important themes in Indian Ocean studies, a zone latticed with "lateral" non-Western interaction and hence a privileged vantage point from which to consider histories of the global south. One strand in this work has been to trace a long history of cosmopolitanism starting with the monsoon- and Muslim-shaped Indian Ocean, interrupted by the age of European empires but resumed through the networks of anti-colonial solidarity that usher in the age of Bandung and notions of Afro-Asian solidarity.

As Burton indicates in her introduction, Indian Ocean studies is one of the historiographical fields in which she locates her work. Yet, as anyone who knows Burton's work, she is a "troubling" historian who disturbs, unsettles, and disrupts any comfort zone or too-easy notions of cosmopolitanism. Whether decentering empire in every possible way or demonstrating the contradictions of white imperial feminism and ideas of global sisterhood, she works with friction, probing the fault line, the contradiction, the limit.

Her project is to bring into view sites of Afro-Asian interaction (often little known, like the community of East African students in India, the result of a post-1947 bursary project started by India to give substance to the ideals of Bandung) while troubling any easy or redemptive accounts of such exchanges. Instead, this book works at the "jagged hyphen" of Afro-Asian solidarity, probing the knotted histories of two zones, tied together in imperial hierarchies of "brown" over "black." "Africa" has long been conscripted as an invisible boundary of Indian nationalism, the "uncivilized" foil to Indic civilization, the bottom tier in a hierarchy of civilizations.

This knotted boundary has largely been overlooked by third-worldist histories that stress fraternity above friction. Burton attempts to capture both in her frame: "Bandung needs to be re-imagined less as an emancipatory lesson than as a cautionary tale about the racial logics in postcolonial states from the moment of their inception: about the enduring power of 'blood and nation.'"[2] As a feminist historian, questions of gender and sexuality are critical in this process:

> "a horizontal network of affiliations rooted in relationships between leaders in the new world of promising postcolonial men, untroubled by conflicts over race, space, women, family or politics." The over-arching intention is to produce histories of as much complexity as possible; to understand "racial difference and conflict as full-bodied dimensions of the postcolonial condition in all its worldly, combative variety, and that . . . resist conscription

by narratives of overcoming, salvation and redemption as well as of solidarity per se."[3]

The method for exploring these themes is configural—the book assembles a series of texts each of which opens up a miniature world where "Africa" and "India" intersect: African-Indian interactions around the anti-apartheid struggle in Durban; the travelogue of Frank Moraes, editor of the *Times of India* of his itinerary through several African countries in 1960; a novel about East African students in Delhi. Any fictional text is itself a miniature configuration, convening a thick description of a world, offering simultaneous forms of insight into that world: psychic, sexual, emotional, semiotic, political, spatial—one could continue indefinitely. As both an acute historian and a gifted literary critic, Burton dissects these novels, listening to the possibilities they open up even while tracing the contradictions in which these become knotted. For her, novels are not simply reflections of the world, they are imaginary attempts to resolve contradictions, to use narrative to settle ambiguity. Her readings of the texts productively mine these fault lines, showing the limits of the ideological projects embodied in each text.

In taking this approach, Burton offers us an experimental method for writing robust histories of the global south, suggesting one set of dots for the reader to join, even as she invites us to think of others. It is a "troubling" and "trouble-making" history, a *tâtonnement*, a tentative and experimental approach to a topic whose complexity this book helps us appreciate.

Notes

1. Ching Kwan Lee, "Raw Encounters: Chinese Managers, African Workers and the Politics of Casualization in Africa's Chinese Enclaves," available at http://www.sscnet.ucla.edu/soc/faculty/CKLee/RawEncounters.pdf, p. 2.

2. *Ibid.*, pp. 6–7.

3. *Ibid.*, pp. 7–8.

Acknowledgments

This book was conceived, researched, and mainly written while I was preoccupied with administrative tasks. There were times I thought that without it and the problems it compelled me to wrestle with, I might have gone under. Parts of various chapters were given as presentations at the Seventh annual Graduate Student South Asia Studies Conference at the University of Chicago, the "Critical Issues in Gender and Transnationalism" symposium at the University of the Witwatersrand, the Center for 21st Century Studies at the University of Wisconsin at Milwaukee, the "Writing the Empire: Scribblings from Below" conference at Bristol, the India International Centre, Delhi University and the Southern African Historical Society, Durban. In each venue I was privileged to have engaged and challenging interlocutors who have helped to shape the outcome. An earlier version of Chapter 1 in a different form appeared in *The Journal of Commonwealth Literature* 46, 1 (2011).

Rajeswari Sunder Rajan first suggested *The Morning After* to me at breakfast several years ago, for which I thank her. With uncanny timing, Ashley Howard pointed me toward *Wizard of the Crow*—part of an exchange of books I hope will long continue. From T. J. Tallie I have had many gifts, including *High Low In-between*, right when I needed it. Meanwhile, Kathy Oberdeck has fed me a steady stream of books from South Africa over the years, and so much more, in ways that have forever shaped me.

Nellie Somers of the Killie Campbell Library in Durban was the first librarian in South Africa I met and she was very good to me. Mwelela Cele not only introduced me to Phyllis Naidoo but took me to see her the first time, for which I will always be grateful. Mrs. Vinoo Reddy of the Gandhi-Luthuli Documentation Centre on the Westville campus of University of KwaZulu-Natal was also gracious, pointing me to the tip of the iceberg of Naidoo's papers there and guiding me through the Centre's other collections. The staff at the School of Oriental and African Studies Library and Archives and at the Institute for Commonwealth Studies, London, was most helpful as well.

There are not enough citations in the world to signal my deep indebtedness to friends and colleagues, near and far. My thanks to Ania Loomba, Minnie Sinha, Uma Dhupelia-Mesthrie, Suvir Kaul, Jed Esty, Dipesh Chakrabarty, Rani Fedson, Sidd Satpathy, Elleke Boehmer, Sukanya Banerjee, Merry Weisner-Hanks, Gerry Forbes, Kumkum Sangari, John Thieme, Fiona Paisley, Kirsty Reid, Julie Parle, Jeff Sahadeo, Renisa Mawani, Melissa Free, Manu Vimalassery, T. J. Tallie, Tony Ballantyne, Anshu Malhotra, Barbara Ramusack, Tanika and Sumit Sarkar, Sanjam Ahluwalia, Malavika Karlekar, Sanjay Joshi, Charu Gupta, Farina Mir, Will Glover, Vinay Lal, Dave Roediger, Rebecca Ginsburg, Terri Barnes, Erik McDuffie, Jim Brennan, Shefali Chandra, Jean Allman, and Dana Rabin for their feedback on bits and pieces of the work and on the scope of the project in general. Isabel Hofmeyr is that rare combination of truly generous and deeply knowledgeable: I feel so indebted to her for her keen eye and unflagging interest. The relay of e-mail between me and her, and between me and Jon Soske, in the last stages of this project have made all the difference. Jon, for his part, freely shared his work, his wisdom, and his tremendous knowledge, modeling deeply ethical scholarship along the way—all this even though we had not met.

Zack Poppel is the most careful and generous of readers, and his own projects have been a veritable inspiration. Debbie Hughes did some legwork for me, which is hugely appreciated, as is Nathan Chio's input. My work with Julie Laut and Irina Spector-Marks to forge something called a "global South Asia" examination field has profited me enormously; Julie shared some passive resistance data with me as well. I've learned so much from Emily Skidmore, for which I will long be indebted. Stuart and Catherine Hall are like beacons and I cannot begin to say how much they have shaped me, intellectually and through the sheer warmth of their company. In Siobhan Somerville I feel lucky to have found a true comrade in the life of the mind. Madhavi Kale is an indispensable reader and beloved friend, as are Herman Bennett and Jennifer Morgan. Angana Chatterji helped connect me to Three Essays Collective and Asad Zaidi has borne our long-distance communications with tremendous grace and generosity. The book is much the better for his interventions. Support from the Bastian funds at the University of Illinois made transnational research possible, for which I am grateful.

To Kathy Oberdeck and William Munro, as well as Fiona and Cara and Wendy and Malcolm, I owe a tremendous debt for introducing me to South Africa, indulging my newcomer questions, and extending themselves on my behalf in untold ways (including much to and froing in and around Durban and on an escape route from an elephant as well). Danielle McFarland has become a mainstay in our lives; without her love, support, and friendship, very little would have gotten done these last five years. My parents and sisters remain stalwarts. Paul and Nick and Olivia are fearless companions in all things, even as they give me the space I need to think and write. There are no words to tell you three how much you mean to me.

And now from citations to salutations. Phyllis and Stuart, Stuart and Phyllis: this book is dedicated to you with loving appreciation, in the hope that you recognize some dimensions of your shared and discrepant struggles, and forgive me for whatever mistakes I have made in seeking to understand them.

Introduction

Citing/Siting Africa in the Indian Postcolonial Imagination

> Race was much more than just a tool of Empire: it was (in the Kantian sense) one of the foundational categories of thought that made other perceptions possible.
> From Ghosh and Chakrabarty, A Correspondence on *Provinclializing Europe*, 2002[1]

> The apparatus is . . . always linked to certain limits of knowledge that arise from it and, to an equal degree, condition it.
> Michel Foucault, *Power/Knowledge* (1980)[2]

Recent attention to the urgency of economic and political cooperation between the Indian government and African states—otherwise known as south-south globalization—suggests that the time has come for new histories of "Afro-Asian solidarity." That term gained currency at the famous meeting of over two dozen Third World representatives in Bandung, Indonesia, in 1955 and refers to the story of affinities and exchanges between people of African and South Asian descent which both ensued from and predated that celebrated marker of postcolonial history. Since then, the term has enjoyed popularity as a metaphor for the fraternal connections between ex-colonial people in the wake of decolonization, when Africans and Indians (and others) joined forces to create a non-aligned movement in contradistinction to the two major superpowers, the USA and the USSR. Bandung and the notion of Afro-Asian solidarity with which it is associated have become touchstones for understanding how postcolonial history unfolded in the Cold War world. Taken together, they are most often cited as the very foundation of postcolonial politics in a global frame.

And yet the term solidarity can be misleading. There is every indication that the terms of endearment between African and Indian communities were strained at best across the landscapes of decolonization. This was true for colonial-born Indians in Durban, for Kenyan students in Delhi and even for politicians like Jawaharlal Nehru and Kwame Nkrumah seeking to navigate the postcolonial world system after 1945. Wherever they shared space, real and imagined, Indians and Africans undoubtedly worked and played together; they also fought with and against each other, sometimes with fatal consequences. *Africa in the Indian Imagination* is an attempt to come to grips with the ins and outs of these relationships, in part by breaking with the redemptive narratives we have inherited from Bandung. Such narratives presume a transracial solidarity *and* a racial confraternity that are belied by the hyphen between Afro and Asian: a hyphen that compresses and elides even as it cuts a variety of ways, ranging from China to Africa to Indonesia, from Kwame Nkrumah to Abdul Nasser to Sukarno to Jawaharlal Nehru. This is especially true when it comes to the question of who was to be on top in the newly postcolonial scene: a pressing issue in a rapidly decolonizing world where racial hierarchies old and new remained consequential to the shape of the postcolonial world order in symbolic and material terms.

As scholars of the period are wont to remind us, there are good reasons for these histories of difference, resentment and suspicion in the Afro-Indian context, among them racialized capitalist relations, colonial-era racial hierarchies, and entrenched practices of racial endogamy.[3] Indeed, the fate of postcolonial power entailed questions of interracial sexuality that were critical to, if not constitutive of, the very idea of Afro-Indian relationships (as they were of nationalist aspirations) in fantasy and in reality. However easily they have tended to slip below the radar of historians and anthropologists, concerns about race mixing between Indians and Africans recast the "inferior" and "superior" bloodline script of colonialism. As they had been before the end of empire, brown-black friendships were danger zones as well as spaces of possibility in the wake of Bandung.[4] How, exactly, we situate Afro-Asian solidarity in the age of Bandung—*how we cite it*—depends on how attentive we are to race, sex and the politics of citation mobilized by a variety of postcolonial writers and activists grappling with the lived experience of, and in, the jagged hyphen. The role of India and Indians in shaping that citationary apparatus and the work of Africa and Africans in shaping Indian postcolonial imaginaries are the chief subjects of this book.

What is a politics of citation? The writers I dwell on here—Ansuyah R. Singh, Francis Moraes, Chanakya Sen (pen name for Bhabani Sen Gupta) and Phyllis Naidoo—routinely call upon Africa and Africans to stake their claims about India or "Indian" politics in the post-1945 period. In so doing they figure Africa as a pillar of Indian identity: a buttress that gives definition to Indianness and that gives Indians, in turn, their local, regional, national, and global significance in the late 20th century world. Despite what we know about the ideological and material work of a tripartite racial system in the pre-postcolonial and post-imperial worlds of India-Africa, whites do not, in the main, enter the frame, and when they do it is not as a centerpiece but rather as an allusive reference. Whether they are working in Durban or Delhi, as journalists or novelists or activists, the writers here rely on Africans either to testify to the coherence of Indian identity in all its gendered, classed, racialized and sexualized dimensions, or to measure the progressive character of Indian political commitments; or both. This shared citationary practice—which takes various discursive forms but typically involves recurrent references to African history, African "personality," African labor and even African sodality—is not simply a recurrent incantation or a nod to a vague set of referents. It is a locative maneuver that serves as a racializing device, positioning Africans as black and Indians as brown, or at the very least as not-African and not-black.[5] To borrow from the feminist theorist Sara Ahmed, it's a mode of representation that tends to racialize as it relegates, locating people of African descent both below Indians in civilizational terms and behind them in temporal terms.[6] One effect of this citing/siting maneuver as the subjects of this book mobilize it is to materialize a set of power relations that are deliberately, insouciantly or accidentally vertical. As such, it enables us to see what we might call a top-down approach to Africa and Africans. It's a verticality that can obtain even when the authors desire, or aspire to, horizontal connections and solidarities.

With the partial exception of Naidoo's work, the presence of Africa and Africans in these writings helps to shore up and consolidate an Indian self dependent on a set of racial/izing hierarchies—a citationary dynamic that points to a larger set of questions about the circulation of Africa, and of blackness, as a trope of the postcolonial Indian imagination. That Naidoo is from a family of indentured workers, and a communist, surely complicates her citationary practice: like many other people of South Asian descent in South Africa of her generation, she expressly rejects polarizing, racialized identities.[7] In South Africa more generally, merchants and "coolies" have had distinctively different relationships with Africans. Here as elsewhere, questions of caste are as indispensable to histories of race as they are to those of gender and sexuality, leaving a differential mark on Afro-Asian possibility depending on by whom and for whom they are articulated.[8] As a grid, "brown over black" in Naidoo's Durban is particularly unstable, reminding us in salutary ways of the impediments to generalization across space and time: reminding us, in short, of the tension between the general case and the specific citation. As important, and because of the dynamism inherent in all systems of power, the effect of the citationary practices I've identified across this book is not necessarily to stabilize racial difference or even to ratify Indian claims to progressive politics. For even when they function as the foundation for new developmental hierarchies, Africa and Africans in the texts under consideration repeatedly demonstrate how structurally dependent Indians were on them for their own political and economic fates, thereby showing up the limits of brown-over-black as a strategy for self-making in the process. If Indians strove to imagine themselves as Indians through disavowal of and/or disidentification with blackness, then, they ended up revealing—often unawares—how thoroughly entangled and profoundly interdependent their stories are with histories of African subjects of all kinds.

Although some attention has been paid to the question of race and South Asian postcoloniality, scholars have tended to think that relationship mainly through references to late 20th century blackness in the US, with African-Americans serving as an index in and for theories about the global economies, symbolic and real, of neocolonialism and minoritization. As Malini Johar Schueller has argued, Homi Bhabha, Arjun Appadurai and Gayatri Spivak have all, with different degrees of specificity, cited African American writers (W.E. B. DuBois, Langston Hughes, Toni Morrison) as evidence of the viability of race as an analytical category for postcolonial politics in ways that invoke a theoretical "world target" yet ultimately redound to an Americo-centric frame.[9] There is a neglected history to these citationary practices, outside the immediate ambit of US power, that we cannot afford to ignore. In each of the essays below I make a case for re-materializing how and why people of South Asian descent in a variety of locations used Africa and Africans as referent points for imagining and consolidating a distinctively Indian identity in a Cold War context where the US was part of a superpower paradigm but was, at least in the 1960s and early 1970s, arguably marginal in and to conceptions of Afro-Asian alignments. Though the authors I focus on are not as famous as the likes of Mohandas Gandhi or Jawaharlal Nehru—figures famous in their own right for siting/citing Afro-Indian connections—they were well known to their contemporaries. Their work is an alternative archive for postcolonial histories that are perhaps over-reliant on the tropes of US racial formation. As such, it offers a contrapuntal history to celebratory accounts of political and affective connection in the age of Bandung.

Of course, histories of Afro-Asian connection predate the 20th century, as Vijay Prashad and others have been at pains to show.[10] There is also a deep history of linkages between African Americans and Indians in 20th century political struggle, what Gerald Horne has called "a lengthy umbilical cord" connecting Black America and post/colonial India.[11] That cord was attached to the makers of US Cold War policy, men who kept a nervous eye on postcolonial events in India and Africa and who had trouble comprehending the nature of Afro-Asian tensions except through crude and mainly undiscriminating comparisons of race and caste.[12] There is no denying the impact of US racial formations on these issues—or, as many scholars have explored, the reverse as well.[13] What I am struck by is how comparatively under-explored the social and cultural history of relationships (political and otherwise) between Indians and Africans actually is, in contrast to the amount of energy that has been spent on tracking a kind of US-global civil rights communitarianism via the analog of race and caste. Even allowing for western prejudices, the fact that contemporary observers felt compelled to puncture the "Bandung myth" by the mid-1960s suggests how overwrought the concept of "a unified, moralizing, crusading Afro-Asia" was—and, to some extent, remains among postcolonial scholars.[14] As Christopher J. Lee and others have shown, the struggle between Afro-Asian nations was on from the very moment of the Bandung itself.[15] If it is to serve as a historiographical pivot, Bandung needs to be re-imagined less as an emancipatory lesson than as a cautionary tale about the racial logics embedded in postcolonial states from the moment of their inception: about the enduring power of "blood and nation," in other words. This is true even and especially when we acknowledge that Bandung invariably casts a long—and as Isabel Hofmeyr and others remind us, a decidedly Indian ocean world—shadow over 21st century histories of the postcolonial condition *tout court*.[16]

One persistent legacy of Bandung is the presumption that racial confraternity was a characteristic feature of "Afro-Asian" experience in its wake: a horizontal network of affiliations rooted in relationships between leaders in the new world of promising postcolonial men, untroubled by conflicts over race, space, women, family or politics. As the work of Elleke Boehmer and Maria Josefina Saldana-Portillo has so persuasively shown, the heroic anti-colonial movement narrative is precisely a masculinist—and a developmentalist—one, shared by colonialists and revolutionaries alike. Boehmer calls this "the syntax of postcolonial nationalism": a kind of grammatical usage akin to citation that is taken up by Nehru, Nkrumah, Nelson Mandela and Benjamin Azikiwe in their movement autobiographies. Following this lead, I suggest that we need more accounts that break from the implicitly fraternal narratives underpinning what remains of the romance of Bandung and by extension, of postcolonial politics in its triumphalist, utopian mode.[17] Relationships between African and Indian men were often fraught, vexed not by racial difference in any essential way but by the ways that political economy, domestic habits and political exigencies gave race fractious meanings across the later 20th century world. Nor were men the only players in "Afro-Asian" contexts: women experienced and participated in these tensions in various capacities, though their histories have been deeply submerged in and by accounts of Bandung. It's time, arguably past time, then, for unsentimentalized histories of cross-racial, interracial community. I seek company with histories that acknowledge racial difference and conflict as full-bodied dimensions of the postcolonial condition in all its worldly, combative variety, and that, frankly, resist conscription by narratives of overcoming, salvation and redemption as well as of solidarity per se.[18]

The point here is not simply to linger on the tensions of Afro-Asian encounter and politics in all their intercontinentality, or to discount the work that Indians and Africans in South Africa and elsewhere did to resist segregation, fight apartheid, or contest the Cold War order in the 1960s and 1970s. Nor is my purpose to excavate or, for that matter, to hypostasize, "Indian" forms of racism or racial thinking. In postcolonial as in colonial contexts, racial logics "were never linear, consistent, or straightforward and were anything but immutable."[19] Rather, I hope to help to nuance the story that students of postcolonial history tell about post-1945 Afro-Asian friendship, and to materialize some of the citationary practices that continue to inform contemporary histories of decolonization during the Cold War.[20] No mere syntactical convenience, the citationary apparatus made visible here—a politics of citation that racializes as it relegates—offers a new vantage point on mid-to-late 20th century histories of India and Africa that requires our critical attention. Such histories are not just genealogies of south-south encounter but, given contemporary political alliances and frictions between Africa and India, they are part of the toolbox of postcolonial geopolitics in all its global ambition as well. With the rise of institutional nodes of exchange and encounter like the Center for Indian Studies in Africa at the University of the Witwatersrand and the Indian Ocean World Centre at McGill, academics north and south and east and west are increasingly part of this complex. As Zeenews. com (an India-based online news source) put it in the run-up to the 2010 World Cup, India and Africa are "joint stock holders in the new emerging dynamics of the world system."[21]

Whereas postcolonial histories have either emphasized Indians' relationship with Britons or have glossed their solidarity with Africans, I argue that concerns about south-south racial and sexual politics need to be (re)integrated into narratives of postcolonial Indian culture and history. Indeed, debates about Africa and India's relationship to it preoccupied postcolonial Indians seeking to be "at home" in an independent nation. One of the tasks of the Nehruvian state was to establish a place for India not simply between two superpowers, but in relationship to the whole of the African continent as well. Nehru echoed the *prima inter pares*, India-over-Africa ethos that had characterized British imperial policy since the late 19th century. For despite his rhetorical support of Afro-Asian solidarity, he did not break entirely from the superstructures of intracolonial interdependence that the British empire had created, and from which India was poised to create a new postcolonial empire, with client states and a set of racialized views of the world beyond independent India. Africa was preeminently subject in this Nehruvian vision of an India-centered world order: a function, perhaps, of the new nationalizing imperatives but a vision with a deeper subcontinental history nonetheless.[22] In the immediate postcolonial period Africa occupied a civilizationally subordinate position in that vision that reports of Mau Mau's "savagery"—cast as expressions of excessively brutalizing black masculinity—could be seen to underscore. If Nehru was one of the architects of the Africa policy of independent India, he was also a carrier of gentlemanly models of statesmanship that contrasted sharply with those of his African contemporaries—like Jomo Kenyatta, whose rough manner and bootstrap past the postcolonial Indian writer Rama Rau invoked to contrast, unfavorably, with Nehru's Harrow/Cambridge education in her coverage of Kenyatta's trial in 1953, on the threshold of Bandung. Such a comparative frame is not expressly racialized, but it suggests what I have elsewhere called "a competitive politics of ... postcolonial masculinity that was threaded through hierarchies of race and class even as it helped to produce, by fixing, those categories themselves."[23] Notably, his particular form of gentlemanliness helps account for the fact that Nehru sketched portraits of his fellow delegates at Bandung for Edwina Mountbatten which included two "hefty and giantly persons" from Gold Coast.[24]

Nor was Nehru by any means the first to have designs on Africa. Though it is little remarked on in recent work on the globality of 1919, the East African Indian National Congress "respectfully" requested the League of Nations to reserve Tanganyika an "Indian" territory "for the purpose of Indian colonization." This came on the heels of massive demonstrations by Indians in Nairobi who favored such a plan. In her presidential address at the EAINC in 1924, Sarojini Naidu supported this colonial ambition for India, arguing that "East Africa . . . is the legitimate Colony of the surplus of that great Indian nation."[25] This recourse to anti-imperial moral authority "which masks a patrician disdain for Africans"—when they are considered at all in the landscape of the African continent, that is—has echoes in Nehruvian geopolitics, especially (though not exclusively) where Indians in South Africa were concerned.[26] We must begin to complement this high geopolitical story with attention to the writing, thinking and political work of "lesser" figures like Singh and Moraes, Sen and Naidoo, so that we can have a richer, fuller picture of what Indians' postcolonial imaginary was, both in and outside India itself. We also need histories of its colonial antecedents, given how dispersed they were across the world, in subimperial regions and supra-regional spaces equally, if distinctively. And here I play, obviously, with the kind of citationary apparatus that privileges some voices over others as the repository of Indian histories, whether regional, national, diasporic or global.[27]

When in the course of working through this project I described it in brief to colleagues, the assumption was that I must be working exclusively on South Africa. Scholars interested in Afro-Asian solidarity have dwelt at length on Gandhi's early South African history, and understandably so. And yet the preoccupation with Gandhi in South Africa also models some of the critical challenges at the heart of my study. For even when historians note his attitudes towards Africans (his use of the pejorative "kaffir," his social and political distance from contemporary African leaders like John Dube, the communalist character of his satyagraha campaign in the Transvaal), there is little recognition that this is but part of a larger story. South African Indians' commitments to anti-apartheid were rooted in powerfully India/n-centered idioms that shored up communal identities and rarely acknowledged the material conditions that subordinated Africans to most if not all Indians in the streets, marketplaces and neighborhoods under the apartheid state and its predecessors. Even less attention is paid to how heteronormative the Gandhian legacy in South Africa is, or how the early satyagraha campaigns depended on notions of Indian women's honor that in turn, played on pollution complexes with race and caste subtexts.[28]

Work that brings all these structural questions into the same frame of analysis is frustratingly rare, for South Africa as elsewhere, and never more so perhaps than where Gandhi is concerned. The sacrality with which his South Africa career tends to be treated, together with an understandable yet nonetheless selective Indian diasporic struggle/heritage narrative, means that seeing both his relations with Africans *and* the landscape of Indian-African relationships more generally is a huge challenge.[29] Indeed, until quite recently, our knowledge of relations between Indians and Africans in places like Durban was much "shadowier" than of those between Indians of different classes. As Jon Soske's work has shown, Indians and Africans mingled in a variety of urban domestic spaces in 20th century Durban, navigating class and race and sexual difference through tense and tender ties. And memoirs like Ismail Meer's testify to the cosmopolitan worlds of early political activities beyond Durban per se, differences of color, class, community and ideology between South Africans notwithstanding.[30]

Yet while our understanding of interaction between Africans and Indians in the inner circles of political activism is becoming fuller, we still need accounts that map its complexities and challenge the endogamy of Indian and African anti-apartheid histories.[31] This is especially true given the way that South Africa is cited in Indian diaspora studies: as a space of racial trauma and triumphant struggle in which Africans are either seen and not heard or assumed to be self-evident comrades in the fight against apartheid. The Passive Resistance campaign of 1946–48 and its assimilation to global narratives of what we might call U.N. postcolonialism—as evidenced by Vijay Lakshmi Pandit's representation of the "South African Indian question"—is critical to this citationary move, though the complex histories of African-Indian relations on the ground in South Africa rarely inform it. Equally critical is the relationship of postcolonial Indian histories to diasporic ones, especially as those terms are variously mobilized by folks in the US, in India, in South Africa and elsewhere. This is a question so huge that I can, alas, only gesture to it here. But it needs to be teased out in the long run if we are to appreciate when Africa gets cited, when it does not; what gets cited as "Indian," what does not; and where, when and under what conditions those citationary moves matter, and for whom.[32]

The asymmetry between Africa as a continent and India as a nation-state is also a huge terminological and conceptual problem. A similar challenge obtains for Durban, both in postcolonial accounts and in this book as well: for just as South Africa is not the whole of the South Asian diaspora in Africa, Durban is also but a slice of the whole as well. Mindful of the selectivity of all citationary apparatus, I take up the conversation by suggesting that even as we acknowledge the work that some Indians did and the sacrifices they made in the 1946–48 South Africa campaign, we must begin to dislodge that story from its pride of place in the interracial romance of Bandung or, at the very least, cite it differently in our narratives of the 1950s and after. As Ansuyah R. Singh's 1960 novel *Behold the Earth Mourns* dramatizes, spaces in which colonial-born Indians and indigenous Africans did coexist in the heat of political struggle were rife with tension and its possibilities: evidence of the yoked histories of Indian and African freedom fighting yet to be fully written, and of the ways that threats to endogamous conjugality helped inexorably to shape them. South Africa is clearly critical to questions of Afro-Asian solidarity, and I have book-ended this volume with two South African writers of Indian descent, beginning with Singh and ending with Phyllis Naidoo's 2002 auto/biographical account of Indian/African relations in the context of the late 20th century anti-apartheid struggle, *Footprints in Grey Street*. Yet even rethinking South Africa in the history of Afro-Asian "solidarity" beyond Gandhi does not tell the whole story of its convulsive histories in the post-1945/post-1947 period. For that we must look to the heart of the subcontinent itself. Whether from the window of an airplane (as in Moraes' 1965 *The Importance of Being Black*) or via the inner chambers of the postcolonial bureaucracy (as in Sen's 1973 novel, *The Morning After*), Africa was on the minds of Indians in India in the decades following independence—in part because Africans were in India proper as students of both Gandhi and "development," in part because the demands of new African states had to be reckoned with in a decolonizing world. Even more mundanely, Africa came to the sightlines of Indians in India through a variety of newspaper accounts, family stories, educational experiences and commercial transactions. This is a phenomenon worth lingering on, given the communities of Africans—Habshis, Sidis—who have peopled India through the centuries and who have been largely elided in general histories of India or in postcolonial accounts of race in/ and India, including those I deal with here.[33] They are part of the politics of color—and of reproduction—that was being worked out in postcolonial India and they merit fuller attention in their own right, as well as alongside the histories of brown over black I am seeking to engage. And while these entanglements remain to be fully historicized for the post-1947 period, let alone for the whole 20th century, Indians were undoubtedly consumers of Africa, literally and figuratively, in many dimensions of their social, political and domestic lives. Even when it took the shape of colonial-born Indians or indentured laborers, "Africa" invaded their dreams, as the vivid images from Subbalakshmi's fragmented, teeming archive so provocatively remind us.[34]

Taken together, what each of the essays here indicates is that the will to a color-blind account of solidarities between Africans and Indians in the service of a transnational or global history of political resistance is in danger of disappearing important and often painful histories of racial dis-ease—histories that were the result of Gandhian legacies, British imperial policies, caste politics and local interactions between communities of color on the ground in various parts of Africa itself. The vertical force of the British empire and its racializing apparatus at multiple levels clearly deserves attention, not least because determining where colonial categories and labor practices end and "local" apprehensions of racial difference and communal identity begin is so notoriously hard. But the embeddedness of that imperial legacy in the global system of a post-1945/post-1947 UN world cannot be discounted either. For it was this interdependent frame—postcolonial but not quite (ever?) post-imperial—that was on the horizon as ex-colonial leaders like Nehru and Kenyatta and Nkrumah all looked ahead to what they knew would be at once discrete and interlinked futures.[35] In this sense, provincializing empire—or, rather, calibrating its historical and explanatory weight with care—is an important challenge for all postcolonial histories.[36]

The visions and the histories that postcolonial nation-states produced have, crucially, been shot through with presumptions, largely unacknowledged, about the link between heteronormativity and the socio-political order. *Africa in the Indian Imagination* aims to historicize the role of Africa and of blackness in the emergence of a postcolonial Indian identity that was both transnational and diasporic, but no less conscious of or invested in racial and sexual difference for being both. Tracking Indians' embrace and disavowal of racial solidarity—what Thomas Blom Hansen calls an "unwieldy fetish"—through articulations of postcolonial sexuality is indispensable for understanding late 20th century ideas about Africa "in the world" and for beginning to historicize the contours of a racially differentiated post-1945 landscape beyond the shadow of western racial formations and as crucially, contiguous with but not contained by US-centric discourses of race.[37] Even allowing for the validity of the claim made by John D. Kelly and Martha Kaplan that "anticolonial movements . . . were a condition of possibility for the success of the American plan for reorganizing the world"—indeed, even allowing for the ways in which many elites and non-elites came to grips with Indian postcolonial history via the example of the US—I want to keep the US in proportion here, because there is much to be gained by re-scaling the role of the US in accounts of postcolonial politics and imagination as well. I take this to be an extension, in fact, of Kelly and Kaplan's call for more careful attention to the specific iterations of US power in the making of the neo-imperial worlds of the late 20th century. Given the ways that historians of the US and South Africa have cited a shared exceptionalism to link histories of Jim Crow and apartheid, taking careful account of the proportionality of American influence and connection seems prudent. Given the traffic, analogical and otherwise, between Dalits and African Americans, doing so is arguably crucial to being able to measure its density against the examples of nationalist/high caste citationary practice I make visible. And given the role of South Africa in that traffic—the centrality it has had in US-based postcolonial narratives of postcolonial history—figuring the impact of American struggles to size might allow us room to see other spaces of Indian-African encounter in diaspora (Uganda, Guyana, Trinidad) more clearly, and to afford them their rightful place in more meaningfully global postcolonial histories as well.[38]

This is not to say that we can or should seek a global narrative of race or diaspora which seeks to draw discrepant histories and contexts into a single frame of analysis—though for some theorists of Asia, globalization represents a kind of non-national alternative that is at once a critique and a legacy of Bandung.[39] I want rather to suggest that postcolonial and diaspora histories might be read as positing a universal story while using specific cases as shorthand—another form of citation—for a set of global conditions that is as variegated as it is, perhaps, ungeneralizable. Nor would I, in offering this interpretive challenge to the normative, masculine, caste Hindu nationalist and apparently racially disinterested subject of postcolonial Indian history, like to be misread as homogenizing either Indians or Africans, brown and black, or as claiming post-1945 India/Africa per se as the only axis along which it is possible to read racialized citations. Still less do I relish being taken to imagine that Indian diasporans were the only ones preoccupied with misrecognition at the site/sight/cite of skin. I am reminded of a story that the founder of Black British Studies, Stuart Hall, told me: when his mother first presented him, newborn, to the family in Jamaica in 1932, his sister, noting his comparatively dark complexion, asked "Where did you get that coolie baby?" And, following up on the story in an interview with Tim Adams in 2007, he explained: "not black baby, you will note, but low-class Indian." And "my father's side was not pure African either, it had Indian in it, and probably some English somewhere."[40] Schemas of brown and black and white and inbetween circulate promiscuously and emerge from very specific conditions of material and symbolic production, of course. The burden of proof about the purchase, and the tenacity, of the particular citationary apparatus I have identified rests on the case studies that follow. Despite the monographic pressures of even a volume of essays like this, whether they add up to anything like portable interpretive framework is, for me, a genuinely, provocatively, open question.

In offering these specific examples, I nonetheless hope to complicate the horizons toward which we tend to look in order to apprehend postcolonial Cold War histories of Afro-Asian connection. Reading vertically, below the sightline of dominant narratives—especially those which privilege Gandhian and/or Nehruvian legacies—gives us an opportunity to engage a variety of histories of the tense and tender relationships between Indians and Africans and, more broadly, of the role of Africa and blackness in the Indian postcolonial imagination. Using fiction and other non-canonical forms of evidence may allow for different kinds of histories than History (capital H) typically ramifies.[41] Think here of M.G. Vassanji's *The In-Between World of Vikram Lall* (2005), Abdulrazak Gurnah's *Desertion* (2005) or Peter Nazareth's *In a Brown Mantle* (1972)—the latter having not simply described Indian life in Uganda but predicted Idi Amin's rise to power and the infamous expulsion of Asians from Uganda, the very same year the novel was published, no less. Think as well, of course, of what Amitav Ghosh has been able to do with India's wide-ranging, cosmopolitan histories in his novels, most recently *Sea of Poppies*. Though far from exceeding the grasp of postcolonial history, these writers seem to know they are not innocent of it either. And they certainly are not: evidence of the work of racism and its endogamous histories leaves its trace in late 20th century in literary work from Africa and India and diaspora equally.[42] Perhaps this is because, as Neville Hoad has written, "in fiction, one can find an archive for the complex lived and felt experience of never completely determining social abstractions"—the abstractions and complexities of postcolonial history no less than any other.[43]

By no means prophets, Singh, Moraes, Sen and Naidoo were well known in their own time as, indeed, they are now in communities closer to home than India proper, perhaps. As I write Naidoo continues to lend her voice to post-apartheid political struggles and to defy its romances and its pieties as well. Indeed, her disavowal of a conventional Indian identity is a provocative challenge to the notion of extra-national belonging—a notion that her account of interracial struggle history arguably queers, and which the term "Afrindian" (to describe the Africanization of Indian selfhood) also evokes.[44] And because her work and that of the others is not widely available beyond university libraries and second-hand bookshops (if there), I have quoted, sometimes at length, from their texts. Even if we concede that they are no more representative of "Indian" opinion or its imaginaries than Gandhi or Nehru, the work of these writers complicates our understanding of the geopolitical landscapes of racial solidarity in late twentieth century considerably. Viewed in the same frame of analysis, their writings illustrate some of the ways that India and people of Indian descent participated in the production of developmentalist narratives which, while borne of western imperial conquest and commercial traffic, continued to accrue to African polities and peoples in the post-war period, shaping not just the fate of emergent states like Kenya, Uganda and Zambia in the so-called Third World arena but that of Africa more generally as a player in the global south as well. Critical to this history was and is the struggle for a culturally particularistic and highly gendered postcolonial Indian self, reliant on the twin consciousness of racial superiority (brown over black) and its correlative, sexual purity (fear of miscegenation), both inside the new nation and beyond it. Inevitably, the scalar frame of such a project is at once local, regional, national, diasporic and global—in part because the history of independent India is a story of racial and sexual politics across shifting boundaries, in part because the terms of that embodied politics helped to shape the spatial parameters of the postcolonial Cold War world.

This project is part of three historiographical turns: one, toward the Indian Ocean world among South Asianists; two, toward histories that link the postcolonial experience and the Cold War among students of the later 20th century; and three, toward analyses that insist on the impact of sexuality and gender in global politics among feminist scholars. Standing as I do at the crossroads of all three, I seek to site/

cite postcolonial histories of Afro-Asian solidarity as manifestations of uneven and competing social, and racial, status between and across extra-national spaces rather than simply as the result of global "flows"—a critical observation derived in part from the work of Africanist anthropologist James Ferguson.[45] Despite the seduction of the horizontal, despite its emancipationist promise, we also have to attend to the historical realities of power relations—what Ahmed, again, calls "the force of the vertical"—which crosscut postcolonial and/or global flows and, in some cases, stopped them in their tracks.[46] Indeed, despite the presumption of transnational connection that has undergirded postcolonial studies, according to Kelly and Kaplan, postcolonial theory itself "tends to diagnose impasse"—impasse thrown up not only by ideas, but by "structures in the world." Even when it produces sparks that nurture collaboration, as it arguably does in the case of Naidoo, this kind of friction is what we should be alert to. As friction, it is akin to what Jasbir Puar calls *conviviality*—that space between the quest for belonging and the exigency of critique.[47]

Such friction produces communities that are no less affective for being fraught with "ugly feelings," no less tightly bound—or historically postcolonial—for being irritative, chafing, edgy, uneasily friendly. Friction is sometimes bloody, sometimes fatal, though never predictably or teleologically so; in any case, it is one of the conditions of fraternity and sorority itself. Which is to say that solidarity can happen through friction; through struggle between and among as well as against; through "tangled, braided... and knotted" lives. *This* is Afro-Asian solidarity in "the grip of worldly encounter"; *this* is the grip of postcolonial critique on the postcolonial past; *this* is the object of my study and the apparently discrepant histories it juxtaposes.[48] This is arguably one of the many yields of feminist postcolonial method as well, especially when it remains open to the possibility that it is not the final word. Nor could it be, given that as method, it leaves its own citationary apparatus—the good, the bad and the ugly—so patently in its wake. I am once again in sync with Sara Ahmed in my desire for histories that have the capacity to estrange us from, as much as attach us to, celebratory, "happy" narratives of the past.[49] This is not because I don't believe solidarities are possible, but because I want us to think our histories of them differently as one method for doing them differently in the contemporary present. As a critique of postcolonial work that presumes a sentimentalized, fraternal history of Afro-Asian solidarity, then, I hope this book offers one example of the form that a critically postcolonial feminist method might take, limitations and all.

Notes

1   Amitav Ghosh and Dipesh Chakrabarty, "A Correspondence on *Provincializing Europe*," *Radical History Review* 83 (2002): 146–172.

2   Cited in Giorgio Agamben, *What is an Apparatus? And Other Essays* (Stanford University Press, 2009), p. 2.

3   Thanks to Jim Brennan for help with this formulation.

4   Viranjini Munasinghe, "Dougla Logics: Miscegenation and the National Imaginary in Trinidad," *South Asian Review* [Special issue on "Empire and Racial Hybridity," edited by Deepika Bhari] 27, 1: 204–32.

5   I am aware of what a volatile and centrifugal term "brown" is: that it has multiple meanings in discrete and discrepant places. Even at the risk of flattening out its contingent meanings and its historicities, I use it heuristically here to connote the uneasy, uneven sense of color difference that a politics of racial citation can illuminate. Nor do I want to suggest that Indians are a homogeneously racialized group, without hierarchies of color embedded in communal identities. I have taken up this question a bit in my work on K.G. Naidoo, the Tamil doctor and anti-apartheid activist, in "The Pain of Racism in the Making of a 'Coolie Doctor,'" *Interventions: International Journal of Postcolonial Studies* 13, 2 (2011): 228 ("the semiotics of Tamil blackness").

6   Sara Ahmed, *Queer Phenomenology: Orientations, Objects, Others* (Durham: Duke University Press, 2006), pp. 3 and 8. For a different use of the citation as device see Russ Castranovo, "'On Imperialism, See . . .': Ghosts of the Present in Cultures of United States Imperialism," *American Literary History* 20, 3 (2008): 427–38.

Introduction ❧ 21

7   For another example from a later generation see Jon Soske, "The Life and Death of Dr. Abu Baker 'Hurley' Asvat, February 23, 1943–January 27, 1989," forthcoming in *African Studies* and provided courtesy of the author.

8   Thanks to Jon Soske for sharpening this point for me. The differential of which I speak is a phenomenon that uncritically Gandhian accounts of Gandhi in South Africa can obscure—for challenges see Maureen Swan, *Gandhi: The South African Experience* (Johannesburg: Ravan Press, 1985) and Sukanya Banerjee, *Becoming Imperial Citizens: Indians in the Late-Victorian Empire* (Durham: Duke University Press, 2010)—and that the life and work of B.R. Ambedkar (1891–1956) throws into bold relief. For a superb feminist/queer account of caste and the making of modern Indian self see Shefali Chandra, *Domesticating English: Sexuality, Caste and the Language of Desire in Modern India* (Duke University Press, forthcoming).

9   Malini Johar Schueller, "Articulations of African-Americanism in South Asian Postcolonial Theory: Globalism, Localism, and the Question of Race," *Cultural Critique*, No. 55. (Autumn, 2003), pp. 35–62. Thanks to Dave Roediger for recommending this essay to me.

10 Vijay Prashad, *Everybody was Kungfu Fighting Afro-Asian Connections and the Myth of Cultural Purity* (Beacon Press, 2002); Dhruba Gupta, "Indian Perceptions of Africa," *South Asia Research* 11, 2 (1991): 158–74.

11 Gerald Horne, *The End of Empires: African Americans and India* (Philadelphia: Temple University Press, 2008), p. 1.

12 Nico Slate, "Translating Race and Caste," *Journal of Historical Sociology* 24, 1 (2011): 70–76.

13 For an excellent account of these impacts, their intellectual and historical power see Kamala Visweswaran, "India in South Africa: Counter-Genealogies for a Subaltern Sociology," in Balmurli Natrajan and Paul Greenough, eds., *Against Stigma: Studies in Caste, Race and Justice Since Durban* (Delhi: Orient Black Swan, 2009), pp. 326–71. The essays in See Seng Tan and Amitav Acharya, eds., *Bandung Revisited: The Legacy of the 1955 Asian-African Conference for International Order* (Honolulu: University of Hawaii Press, 2009) nicely summarize and re-orient "what actually happened" at Bandung, as well as before and after (quote is Itty Abraham, "Bandung and State Formation in Post-colonial Asia," p. 48).

14 G.H. Jansen, *Non-Alignment and the Afro-Asian States* (New York: Praeger, 1966), p. 248; [no author], *Afro-Asian Solidarity Against Imperialism: A Collection of Documents, Speeches and Press Interviews from the Visits of Chinese Leaders to Thirteen African and Asian Countries* (Peking: Foreign Language Press, 1964); and Jamie Mackie, *Bandung 1955: Non-Alignment and Afro-Asian Solidarity* (Singapore: Editions Didier Millet, 2005).

15 Christopher J. Lee, ed., *Making a World After Empire: The Bandung Moment and its Political Afterlives* (Athens: Ohio University Press, 2010).

16 For "blood and nation" see See John D. Kelly and Martha Kaplan, *Represented Communities: Fiji and World Decolonization* (Chicago: University of Chicago Press, 2001), esp. chapter 3 (on Fiji and Hawaii); and Pamila Gupta, Isabel Hofmeyr and Michael Pearson, eds., *Eyes Across the Water: Navigating the Indian Ocean* (Pretoria: UNISA, 2010).

17 Elleke Boehmer, "The Hero's Story: The Male Leader's Autobiography and the Syntax of Postcolonial Nationalism," in her *Stories of Women: Gender and Narrative in the Postcolonial Nation* (Manchester: Manchester University Press, 2005), pp. 66–87 and Maria Josefina Saldana-Portillo, *The Revolutionary Imagination in the Americas and the Age of Development* (Durham: Duke University Press, 2003). I am grateful to Manu Vimalassery for re-animating this book for me. See also Vijay Prashad, "Amitava Kumar's Excellent Adventure," *Z Space*, July 3, 2007. http://www.zcommunications.org/amitava-kumars-excellent-adventure-by-vijay-prashad (last accessed September 21, 2010) and Antoinette Burton, "The Sodalities of Bandung: Toward a Critical 21st Century History" in Lee, ed., *Making a World After Empire*, pp. 351–361.

18 I am indebted here to David Scott, *Conscripts of Modernity: The Tragedy of Colonial Enlightenment* (Durham: Duke University Press. 2004); in many ways, citation functions for me as conscription does for him.

19 Renisa Mawani, *Colonial Proximities: Crossracial Encounters and Juridical Truths in British Columbia, 1871–1921* (Vancouver: UBC Press, 2009), p. 12.

20 Thanks to Jon Soske for urging me to think carefully about this question.

21 For assessments of a variety of contemporary India-African cooperation projects (including in Sudan, Ethiopia and North Africa) see Ajay Dubey, ed., *Trends in Indo-African Relations* (New Delhi: Manas Publications [in collaboration with the African Studies Association of India], 2010); for zeenews see http://www.zeenews.com/FIFAWC2010/story.aspx?aid=634703; last accessed March 2011. Despite even the critique of "Africa chic" in China, the literature on China in Africa does not presume romance; see Chris Alden, *China in Africa: Partner, Competitor or Hegemon?* (London, Zed Books, 2007); Ali Askouri et al., *African Perspectives on China in Africa* (Pambazuka Pres, 2007); and Firoze Manji and Stephen Marks, ed., *African Perspectives on China in Africa* (Cape Town: Fahuma, 2007).

22 Thanks to Isabel Hofmeyr for insisting on this; see also Gupta, "Indian Perceptions."

23 Antoinette Burton, *The Postcolonial Careers of Santha Rama Rau* (Duke University Press, 2007), p. 64.

24 Cited in Judith M. Brown, *Nehru: A Political Life* (New Haven: Yale University Press, 2003), p. 261. For more detail on contemporaries' views of Nehru see Dipesh Chakrabarty, "The Legacies of Bandung: Decolonization and the Politics of Culture," in Lee, ed., *Making a World*, p. 49 and Rahul Mukherji, "Appraising the Legacy of Bandung: A View from India," in Tan and Acharya, eds., *Bandung Revisited*, p. 169.

25 Cited in Gupta, "Indian Perceptions," p. 163. The rest of the quote is: "I stand, therefore, today before you as an Indian speaker on Indian soil—that your forefathers have dug—cities that your forefathers have built in a land which your ancestors gave to the cities of the country—citizens by the right of heredity, citizens by the right of tradition, citizens by the right of patriotic love which has been nurtured, fostered and developed by the sweat of the brow and the blood of the heart of the pioneers exiled from India, so that Indian interests may grow greater." Indian workers are visible here, though there is nary an African in sight. See also Robert Gregory, *India and East Africa: A History of Race Relations within the British Empire, 1890–1939* (Oxford: Oxford University Press, 1971).

26 My thanks to Isabel Hofmeyr for helping me map this formulation; see her "Universalizing the Indian Ocean," PMLA 125, 3 (2010): 721–9 and her "The Idea of 'Africa' in Indian Nationalism," *South African Historical Journal* 57 (2007): 60–81. Even the Indian princes had an eye on Africa; according to Barbara Ramusack, "In February 1917 the maharaja [Ganga Singh] of Bikaner wrote to Lord Chelmsford requesting that the princes be given land grants, in India or in conquered areas abroad such as German East Africa, as rewards for their war services as had been done in appreciation for princely support during the Revolt of 1857." See her *The Princes of India in the Twilight of Empire: Dissolution of a Patron-client System, 1914–1939* (Columbus: Ohio State University Press, 1978), p. 61.

27 I've dealt with the question of "minor" writers in *The Postcolonial Careers of Santha Rama Rau*. For Ramayana colonialism see John D. Kelly, "Fiji's Fifth Veda: Exile, Sanatan Dharm and Countercolonial Initiatives in Diaspora," in Paula Richman, ed., *Questioning Ramayanas: A South Asian Tradition* (Berkeley: University of California Press, 2000), pp. 329–51.

28 Thanks to Shefali Chandra for pressing me on some of these points, which I deal with in greater length in Chapter 1; see Radhika Mongia, "Gender and the Historiography of Gandhian *Satyagraha* in South Africa," *Gender & History* 18, 1 (2006): 130–149 and Goolam Vahed, "The Making of 'Indianness': Indian Politics in South Africa During the 1930s and 1940s," *Journal of Natal and Zulu History* 17 (1997): 1–36.

29 This is true beyond the case of South Africa as well of course: see http://www.thehindu.com/news/national/article1597266.ece (last accessed April 2011).

30 "Shadowier" is Bill Freund's term. See his *Insiders and Outsiders: The Indian Working Class of Durban, 1910–1990* (London: James Currey, 1995), p. 38. See also Jon Soske, "Navigating Difference: Gender, Miscegenation and Indian Domestic Space in 20th century Durban" in Gupta et al, *Eyes Across the Water*, pp. 197–219; Ismail Meer, *A Fortunate Man* (Cape Town: Zebra Press, 2002); and Nelson Mandela, *Long Walk to Freedom* (Boston: Little Brown, 1994). "Tense and tender ties" evokes Ann Laura Stoler, "Tense and Tender Ties: The Politics of Comparison in North American History and (Post) Colonial Studies," *Journal of American History* 88, 3 (2001) and her edited collection, *Haunted by Empire: Geographies of Intimacy in North American History* (Durham: Duke University Press, 2006).

31 For ethnographic studies of such contact in the Caribbean see Aisha Khan, *Callaloo Nation: Metaphors of Trace and Religious Identity among South Asians in Trinidad* (Durham: Duke University Press, 2004); Tejaswini Niranjana, *Mobilizing India: Women, Music and Migration between India and Trinidad* (Durham: Duke University Press, 2006); and Munasinghe, "Dougla Logics," 204–32. For calls for attention to the yoked histories of Indians and Chinese in South Africa, see Karen L. Harris, "Gandhi, the Chinese and Passive Resistance" in Judith M. Brown and Martin Prozesky, eds., *Gandhi and South Africa: Principles and Politics* (New York: St. Martin's Press, 1996), pp 69–94 and Melanie Yap and Dianne Leong Mann, *Colour, Confusion and Concessions: The History of the Chinese in South Africa* (Hong Kong University Press, 1996).

32 For an excellent set of reflections on this see the special issue of *South African Historical Journal* 57 (2007), especially the Isabel Hofmeyr and Uma Duphelia-Mesthrie, "South Africa/India: Re-Imagining the Disciplines," pp. 1–11. For a methodological approach that upends the time/space frame of diaspora and nation see John D. Kelly and Martha Kaplan, "Diaspora and Swaraj, Swaraj and Diaspora," in Dipesh Chakrabarty, Rochona Majumdar and Andrew Sartori, eds., *From the Colonial to the Postcolonial: India and Pakistan in Transition* (New Delhi: Oxford University Press, 2007), pp. 311–31.

33 Thanks to Madhavi Kale for pressing me on this point. See Shihan de Silva Jayasuriya and Jean-Pierre Angenot, eds., *Uncovering the History of Africans in Asia* (New York: Brill, 2008); Kenneth X. Robbins and John McLeod, eds., *African Elites in India: Habshi Amarat* (Ahmedabad: Mapin, 2006); Shihan de Silva Jayasuriya & Richard Pankhurst, eds., *The African Diaspora in the Indian Ocean* (Trenton, NJ : Africa World Press, 2001); and Shanti Sadiq Ali, *African Dispersal in the Deccan: From Medieval to Modern Times* (London: Sangam, 1996).

34 Mythily Sivaram, *Fragments of a Life: A Family Archive* (New Delhi: Zubaan, 2007), pp. 143–49. In her case the image is of a Tamil servant woman, not an African. Thanks to Urvashi Butalia for this reference.

35 I draw here on John D. Kelly and Martha Kaplan, "'My Ambition is Much Higher than Independence': US Power, the UN World, the Nation-State and their Critics," in Prasenjit Duara, ed., *Decolonization: Perspectives from Now and Then* (New York: Routledge, 2004), pp. 131–151.

36 I have addressed this question for British imperial history per se in an essay called "Getting Outside the Global: Re-Positioning British Imperialism in World History," in Catherine Hall and Keith McLelland, eds., *Race, Nation and Empire: Making Histories, 1750 to the Present* (Manchester: Manchester University Press, 2010), pp. 199–216.

37 Thomas Blom Hansen, "The Unwieldy Fetish: Desire and Disavowal of Indianness in South Africa," in Gupta et al., *Eyes Across the Water*, pp. 109–21. This is something akin to what John Hawley, citing Gwenda Vender Steele, suggests about the ongoing Indian-African relationship vis a vis Europe and America today. See Hawley, ed., *India in Africa, Africa in India: Indian Ocean Cosmopolitanisms* (Bloomington: Indiana University Press, 2008), p. 7.

38 Kelly and Kaplan, "'My Ambition,'" pp. 141, 144. I'd include the postcolonial studies world, which is notoriously considered to be about the non-west from the location of the west, in this formulation. For one of the best diagnoses of this question see Paul T. Zeleza, "Historicizing the Posts: The View from African Studies," in Zine Magubane, ed., *Postmodernism, Postcoloniality and African Studies* (Trenton, NJ: Africa World Press, 2003), pp. 1–38. For dalit-African American traffic see Visweswaran, "India in South Africa"; Vijay Prashad, "Afro-Dalits of the World, Unite!" *African Studies Review* 43, 1 (2000): 189–201 and his http://www.nondomesticatedthinker.com/2010/03/the-story-of-an-afro-dalit-of-india/ (last accessed March 2011); and Gyanendra Pandey "The Politics of Difference: Reflections on the African American and Dalit Struggles," *Economic and Political Weekly* XLV, 19 (May 2010). Thanks as ever to Jon Soske for helping me think this through, and to Herman Bennett for his insight as well.

39 See Hee-Yeon Cho, "Revitalizing the Bandung Spirit," in Kuan-Hsing Chen and Chua Beng Huat, eds., *The Inter-Asia Cultural Studies Reader* (London: Routledge, 2007), p. 585. Adeke Adebajo sees the end of apartheid in 1994 as "the culmination of Bandung." See his "From Bandung to Durban: Whither the Afro-Asian Coalition," in Tan and Acharya, eds., *Bandung Revisited*, p. 105.

40 For a fuller account see Stuart Hall, David Morley, Kuan-Hsing Chen, *Stuart Hall: Critical Dialogues in Cultural Studies* (Psychology Press, 1996), p. 487; and Tim Adams, "Cultural Hallmark," *The Guardian* 23 September, 2007.

41 See Antoinette Burton, *Dwelling in the Archive: Women Writing House, Home, and History in Late Colonial India* (New York: Oxford University Press, 2003).

42 Elleke Boehmer, "Without the West: 1990s Southern Africa and Indian Woman Writers—A Conversation?" *African Studies* 58, 2 (1999): 157–14; Simon Gikandi and Evan Mwangi, *The Columbia Guide to East African Literature in English since 1945* (New York: Columbia University Press, 2007), p. 111; Amitav Ghosh, *Sea of Poppies* (London: John Murray, 2008); and Abdulrazak Gurnah, "Imagining the Postcolonial Writer," in Susheila Nasta, ed., *Reading the 'New' Literatures in a Postcolonial Era* (DS Brewer, 2000), pp. 73–86.

43 Neville Hoad, *African Intimacies: Race, Homosexuality and Globalization* (Minneapolis: University of Minnesota Press, 2007), p. 22.

44 Pallavi Rastogi, *Afrindian Fictions: Diaspora, Race and National Desire in South Africa* (Columbus: Ohio State University Press, 2008).

45 James Ferguson, *Global Shadows: Africa in the Neoliberal World Order* (Durham: Duke University Press, 2006), especially the introduction and chapters 1 and 7.

46 Ahmed, *Queer Phenomenology*, p. 159.

47 Kelly and Kaplan, "Diaspora and Swaraj, Swaraj and Diaspora," in Chakrabarty, Majumdar and Sartori, eds., *From the Colonial to the Postcolonial*, p. 311; Jasbir Puar, *Terrorist Assemblages: Homonationalisms in Queer Times* (Durham: Duke University Press, 2007), p. xiv.

48 See Mawani, *Colonial Proximities*, p. 203; Leela Gandhi, *Affective Communities: Anticolonial Thought, Fin-de-Siecle Radicalism and the Politics of Friendship* (Durham: Duke University Press, 2006) and Sianne Ngai, *Ugly Feelings* (Cambridge: Harvard University Press, 2007). For metaphors of friction and grip I borrow from Anna Lowenhaupt Tsing, *Friction: An Ethnography of Global Connection* (Princeton: Princeton University Press, 2005).

49 Thanks to Minnie Sinha for reminding me that the story nonetheless remains open to new research, interpretation and conclusions. For the dilemma of the citation and its reproductive capacities, see Mieke Bal, "The Politics of Citation," *diacritics* 21, 1 (1991): 25–45, which is a review of three books on racial images in postcards, painting and other colonialist iconography. For happiness see Sara Ahmed, "Killing Joy: Feminism and the History of Happiness," *Signs: Journal of Women in Culture and Society* 35, 3 (2010): 571–574. I am grateful to Siobhan Somerville for taking me back to this essay.

Chapter 1

"Every Secret Thing"?

Racial Politics in Ansuyah R. Singh's *Behold the Earth Mourns* (1960)

the border

*is as far
as the black man
who walks alongside you*

*as secure
as your door
against the unwarranted knock*

Shabbir Banoobhai, 1980[1]

The history of Indians in South Africa turns on several racialized axes at once. The consolidation of a common "settler" identity derived from racially discriminatory treatment under both the colonial and the apartheid state was always already shaped by anxieties about proximity to, and dependence on, Africans. Acknowledgement of these multiple axes requires us to concede that a plurality of racisms undergirds Indians' experiences in South Africa, and that communal identity, albeit fragmented across a range of ethnic and caste differences, operates at least in part as a racializing device.[2] In the context of mid- to late 20th century anti-apartheid politics in South Africa, it also means that we must reconcile a robustly, if contingently, racialized

Indian identity with the emergence of a set of cross-racial[3] political commitments among a small but influential set of South Africans of South Asian descent. The events of 1946–1948 epitomize the multi-axial, multiply moving parts of South African racial politics. These years, among the best documented in the historiography of Indians in South Africa, witnessed the mass mobilization of Indians in a passive resistance movement against racially discriminatory laws aimed at displacing their communities from permanent and self-selected settlement *and* gave rise to the first organized non-European "united front" activities in South Africa—with international ramifications in the short and long term for universal human rights on a global scale. Rather than being incommensurate, the experience of racial identity as Indians and an awareness of the urgency of cross-racial alliances together became the presumptive, if unstable, ground of anti-apartheid politics for those Indians who embraced it in the late 1940s.[4]

Scholars and activists interested in building a variety of historical narratives about anti-apartheid work have had, inevitably, to cite this watershed moment, though most do not linger on the concrete details of why and under what circumstances cross-racial alliances were forged between Indians and Africans. Those who have been concerned with accounting for how (or whether) a cross-racial anti-apartheid movement in South Africa developed in the wake of Indian settler protest have focused on institutional and organizational sources, drawing on memoirs and autobiographical reflections where available—or, as Jon Soske does, on the evidence of shared urban spaces to be found in newspapers like *Drum* and *Ilanga Lase Natal*.[5] As a counterpoint and a contribution to that historiography, I read Ansuyah Singh's novel, *Behold the Earth Mourns*, as a critical history of anti-apartheid struggle in the latter half of the 20th century. Published in 1960, Singh's novel chronicles the birth of personal and political consciousness among those Indians in mid-century Durban who fought a variety of punitive and racially exclusionary laws aimed at suppressing their livelihoods and driving them from the country. It has been hailed as the first novel written by a South African Indian and, in the context of the new South Africa, it is well on its way to being cited as, and assimilated to, a new generic category: struggle literature in the service of heritage history.[6] This phenomenon has been especially visible in the context of 2010 which, in addition to witnessing the World Cup in South Africa, was also the 150th anniversary of the arrival of the first Indian indentured laborers to Natal and the beginning of an organized scheme to deliver what would be tens of thousands of Indian workers to the sugar cane fields of South Africa. A return to Singh's novel in the wake of the sesquicentenary of Indian arrival serves a recovery agenda and a pedagogical purpose for those who, like Devarakshanam Govinden, seek to "reclaim" it for its contribution to "the possibilities for reconsider[ing] . . . the politics of identity for a readership grappling with different challenges from those of the 1950s and 1960s."[7]

Less well attended to is the role of African characters in shaping the plot structure of *Behold the Earth Mourns*: the citationary apparatus whereby they enter the novel's history of passive resistance. Though Govinden refers in passing to Singh's treatment of Indian/African interactions, she focuses mainly on the Indian communal story and its links to the Indian subcontinent. She takes up the question of the novel's racial politics by juxtaposing it with other "black" writing before and after its publication or by reminding us of the anti-apartheid struggles unfolding at the time of its publication—strategies of reading and citation I will return to at the end of my essay. Borrowing from the critical framework afforded by Toni Morrison's *Playing in the Dark*, I take the landscape of Singh's novel not as a monochromatic surface across which Indians travel, self-contained, toward political consciousness but as highly racialized topography through which Indians move in concert and sometimes in collision with Africans who, in turn, have a consequential impact on the central plot and on the characters' development in the story.⁸ Rather than erupting intermittently along the plotline, in other words, the African characters in *Behold the Earth Mourns* serve as its superstructural apparatus, its footnotes: they are integral and even indispensable to its forward (and backward) motion—referencing deep genealogies of politics and establishing the epistemological foundations for political action, even resistance. Re-materializing the *interracial* modes of engagement on view in the novel via the citationary apparatus that it employs not only destabilizes the story of progressive Indian political development, it helps to underscore the multidimensionality of racial formation in South Africa to which I referred at the start—brown and black, brown over black and even occasionally black over brown—and to complicate the relationship between fiction and politics. And when we consider how the novel's racial politics are embodied in gendered terms we begin to appreciate the political challenges of a critically engaged feminist historical reading as well.

I am emphatically *not* making a case for the novel as an example of interracial harmony but as a site where interracial interaction—and even co-dependence—has been both cited and archived. Insisting on the material presence of Africans in this fictional account of an Indian merchant family in 1940s South Africa by reading for them and through as actors and agents rather than simply as subjects below the plotline helps to nuance our histories of the development of a self-consciously racialized Indian settler identity which was dependent—in economic, political and imaginative terms—on the literal and figurative work of the indigenous African, and on a set of heteronormative anxieties and aspirations that framed that dependence. Though each of those categories (Indian, African, settler, native, heteronormative) is scarcely monolithic, I compress them here heuristically, for the sake of argument. My aim here is to think *Behold the Earth Mourns* beyond the bounds of recovery history: to challenge its function as struggle literature only about or for Indians of South African descent and in so doing, to re-purpose it for conversations about how to write and how to read histories of Indo-African connection from the 20th century in the 21st.

The Indian Marriage Plot; or, Making Satyagraha Histories

One hundred years after the arrival of the first indentured Indians in South Africa, Ansuyah R. Singh (1917–1978) published her first novel, *Behold the Earth Mourns*. It tells the story of the transnational marriage between a Bombay woman, Yagesvari Jivan-Sinha, and a Durban man, Srenika Nirvani. Srenika's father arrived not as an indentured laborer but as a trader who eventually accumulated enough capital to start a small sugar cane farm himself, which would grow as the city took off in the 20th century. Yagesvari, for her part, comes from a well-to-do, cosmopolitan "modern" urban Indian family. The tale of their marriage is set against the tumultuous 1940s, when the incursions of the state into the lives and livelihoods of Indian settlers compelled young men like Srenika into the streets of Durban and Cape Town and Port Elizabeth to protest the Asiatic Land Tenure and Indian Representation Bill (1946). Known popularly as the Ghetto Act, the bill limited the rights of Indians to own or occupy land. It is considered "a landmark in the history of the South African freedom struggle," not least because it galvanized public opinion among Indians in India as well as people of South Asian descent in Africa around the "South African Indian question"—that is, the racial discrimination to which Indian communities in South Africa were subject with increasing ferocity on the threshold of the first National Party government in 1948. Both Gandhi and the working committee of the Indian National Congress joined the South African Indian Congress in a call to oppose the legislation and threatened that if the Smuts government did not suspend it, they would organize a roundtable conference "to consider the whole policy of the Union Government against non-white peoples of the earth."⁹ The Ghetto Act nonetheless became law, the Natal and the Transvaal Indian Congresses established Passive Resistance Councils (PRCs), and Indians went to jail by the hundreds for their protest efforts. Especially because of its embrace by Gandhi, but also because of its ideological work in raising transnational consciousness about the fate of Indians in South Africa, in the annals of South African Indian history the passive resistance movement is considered the "Glorious" start to the anti-apartheid struggle of the next five decades.¹⁰

Srenika's politicization in response to discriminatory legislation, his involvement in passive resistance demonstrations, his imprisonment and his awakening to the ways of the world that result from his political activity—all are emblematic of the coming of age of an entire generation of colonial-born Indians of his class in the 1940s. From the start we witness the pain of Srenika's discovery of racial injustice and his transformation into a street protester, specifically over the question of Indians' right to land and to settlement, now threatened by news of evictions being visited on local people. As he tells his brother Krishandutt, "it is because you have another place to go to—one here, another there, it does not upset you. But what about the other people? Have you ever thought of them? It is all they have got. They are not cattle, nor sheep that you can move from one grazing land to another. Don't you feel . . . the aura of mystery, the sanctity, the precious meaning of our home, of their home . . . ?"¹¹ Krishandutt is a ready foil to Srenika: he chooses reason over emotion—he is the oldest son, in charge of the family business—and pragmatism over rash action. While he has been "bent over his writing desk, absorbed in his accounts and ledgers," Srenika has been studying government policy and turning a critical eye not just on colonial power but on his family's enterprise as well. He rebukes his brother for focusing on profit, reflecting that "all the laws, the cancerous plans could go on as long as it did not touch him, his family and business. How long did he expect to be untouched?"¹²

Krishandutt acknowledges that their own father had suffered "all the jibes, hurt and humiliation" of being Indian in South Africa, but reminds Srenika that he chose charity for the less fortunate through provisions for a school, beds in hospitals and support for local newspapers. Srenika expressly rejects this route as "soft, sitting back and hoping for something to change." He, in turn, reminds Krishandutt of the stakes of resistance for his own family, recalling how Krishandutt's daughter was seriously injured but had had to wait because parts of the hospital she went to for treatment were for Europeans only. "The whole structure of this system is based on a menacing wrongness. You cannot demand restraint from me . . . my being, the whole of me cannot." With that Krishandutt turns to his wife and announces ruefully, "Srenika . . . is becoming a Satyagrahi."[13]

Given the longstanding class and caste tensions in the South African Indian community over the question of how, or whether, to resist to colonial authority at the site of law, Singh's staging of the brothers' quarrel is a useful window into the affective dimensions of internecine political struggle. Though it is less well known outside South African historiography, Gandhi's arrival in South Africa in the 1890s and his own satyagraha efforts there up to 1913 created and exacerbated deep divisions between merchant capitalist interests and more radical groups over the nature and benefit of collective opposition to punitive, state-sponsored anti-Indian legislation.[14] The split in philosophy and tactics that unfolds at the start of the novel captures differences that might well have played out across families in Durban in this period, if not also within them as well. Srenika's decision to join the protesters and his subsequent arrest and imprisonment were not untypical for Indians of his class and generation; among the most prominent of the passive resisters in 1946–48 was K.G. Naidoo, whose family also began as traders and whose medical training at Edinburgh (she had a lifelong career as a doctor as "Dr. Goonam") arguably placed her in a different class position, in cultural if not in strictly economic terms, than her family of origin.[15] Of note too is that Srenika's route into passive resistance is via Christ and Buddha as well as Gandhi, as his manifesto on non-violence testifies:

> Friends: It is with great happiness that I court imprisonment today in the true spirit of Satyagraha. Passive resistance owes its origins to the deep fundamental truth of Hindu philosophy. It has the foundation of the teaching of Christ and Buddha. It is a truth, a love force endeavouring to uphold non-violence, for violence and force have never solved any problems. They never will. Force must not be used to redeem our freedom as a free people amongst the nations of the world. We believe only in making our cause felt by physical suffering. After deep and serious thought, I have come to the conclusion that there comes a time when the spirit rebels against a way of life based on exercised superiority. Timid and passive acquiescence makes it possible to strengthen this superiority... the popular road is the path of revolution and violence. If it is bloodshed and massacre—slaughter of the maligned against the maligning, there is insanity. There is no victory for either... The road of non-violence is harder. It is a disciplined mastery of the physical, emotional and spiritual forces of passivity against any wrong."[16]

As a declaration of passive resistance, this manifesto captures the ecumenism of Gandhian satyagraha as well as its promontory view of "the popular," with its equation of revolution and insanity. Given that the African National Congress at this stage was hostile to passive resistance as a strategy, Srenika is carving out not just a political or even a communal identity for himself but a distinctively, if implicitly, racialized one as well.

But if Srenika's political education is the point of departure for the novel, it is his marriage to Yagesvari upon which the rest of the plot turns. In many respects, given his family of birth, his class/caste status and the heteronormative exigencies of both, marriage was always his destination. As he tells Krishandutt, prison "jolted me into maturity"—a jolt that propelled him not toward ongoing political activity in the organizational sense, but directly toward a choice of bride. Having chosen marriage as the next step—into "maturity" and presumably "beyond" politics—Srenika finds himself at the heart of the politics of conjugality in South Africa. As he tries to start a new life with his Indian wife, he discovers that she is barred from entering the country, thanks to a law targeting the mobility of Indian women, and specifically wives, from India to South Africa. What had been largely rhetoric on Srenika's part is now brought dramatically into his own prospective marriage bed. Yagesvari asks for an entry permit and she is granted one, in part by appealing to the border guard. Living under the constant cloud of secrecy and fear of discovery, they manage nonetheless to conceive a child, and Yagesvari returns to India to have a baby girl, Malini. Unable to bear the separation, she returns to South Africa with a passport. In a somewhat confusing scene, she and Malini are ushered off the boat by a friend, and go into hiding outside the city. Eventually Malini is released, leaving a despondent Yagesvari in jail. She attempts suicide and is also eventually released, very unwell, and they live in anxiety because the decision about whether she can by law remain with Srenika remains unresolved. Though it is not expressly stated at the end of the novel, the implication is that she dies broken in body and in spirit by the ordeal, effectively, of her married life.

The political re-education of Srenika occurs through the experience of conjugality thwarted, even denied, by racist legislation aimed precisely at managing Indian reproduction, sexual, demographic and otherwise. This is where Singh's work commands our attention, in the first instance, as more than just an ordinary history of the politics of the 1940s. The collision of the couple's marriage plans with these historical events not only shapes the lives of Srenika and Yagesvari, it marks the struggles over race, settlement and "Indianness" as a crisis of conjugality and family life, singling out the body and the experience of the Indian woman as the very grounds of Indian politics and identity in South Africa. It's easy enough to see how un/cannily Singh anticipated the work of Gayatri Spivak and Lata Mani, whose arguments about Indian women serving as the pretext for debates between colonized and colonizing men over the nature and extent of patriarchal power have become staples of postcolonial feminist criticism.[17] As significantly, *Behold the Earth Mourns* rehearses an underexplored but critical history of resistance and marriage and communalism in early 20th century South Africa, notably Gandhi's own satyagraha campaign in South Africa in 1913. Although the occasion for that movement was ostensibly the L3 tax imposed on indentured labors who wished to buy themselves out of their contracts, questions of marriage were entailed in that struggle as well. The Searle decision of 1913, which was issued in response to the petition by Hassan Essop that his wife not be deported, for all intents and purposes nullified non-Christian and/or non-registered marriages, threatening the respectability and the very viability of Indian family life in South Africa at a time when it was already tenuous at best, in both economic and political terms.[18]

According to Radhika Mongia, whose work has sought to re-center both gender and conjugality in the history of satyagraha in South Africa, it was nothing less than "the gendered discourse of national honor" mobilized around the Searle decision that enabled the 1913 non-violent movement to unfold across what was "a fractured social field" in Indian communities at the time.[19] Without it, she implies, Gandhi's first experiment in mass civil disobedience might never have gotten off the ground. The 1913 demonstrations included Indian women, who transgressed any number of customary prescriptions to march and in so doing, rejected notions that they could only be the objects of political discourse rather than agents of political action. *Behold the Earth Mourns* echoes and arguably retells this earlier history, threading it through more recent memory and underscoring in the process the centrality of Indian women, and their bodily suffering/sacrifice, to the politics of resistance on the threshold of institutionalized apartheid. To be sure, Singh did not have to return to the grid of 1913 to link passive resistance with the conjugal choices of the Indian merchant community in Durban or elsewhere in South

Africa. She herself was active in the campaign, a first-hand observer of the politics of the events surrounding it.[20] And the law monitoring the passage of Indian women from India to South Africa which throws Srenika's family plans into chaos is not fictionalized. But like the story Mongia tells about 1913, it is also not a dominant or even well-known dimension of the 1946–48 passive resistance movement that Singh dramatizes in *Behold the Earth Mourns*. And although women famously took to the streets in 1946, and their activities have been chronicled both by those who were there and by scholars and activists seeking to underscore Indian women's public role in anti-apartheid struggles, Singh's novel is arguably unique for the attention it draws to the impact of racist legislation on the innermost recesses of the Indian household, home, family in the context of this passive resistance campaign.

Though it is little remarked on, Singh's own work as a medical doctor—like Goonam, she studied at Edinburgh and practiced both in the UK and in South Africa—brought her face to face with the effect of poverty and dispossession on the Indian community. She was the co-author of a scientific article in 1960, the same year her novel was published, called "Antenatal Stress and the Baby's Development"—a study based on interviews with over 100 women in a Durban suburb via the Institute of Family and Community Health done between 1959–60. All the women were of South Asian descent, and the article tracks the impact of stressors ("the unemployment or partial employment of the husband, and distress at being pregnant, usually in conjunction with straitened economic circumstances") on several aspects of babies' health, including birth weight and attachment to the mother.[21] In fact, the article places as much emphasis on the mother as on the baby, which may be an indication that the writing of the character Yagesvari was influenced by her medical practice, or vice versa. Though Srenika and Yagesvari's daughter Malini are perfectly healthy, it's possible to read Yagesvari's decline as a kind of post-partum depression and suicide attempt triggered by the trauma of imprisonment, separation from child and family and ongoing fear for her own safety and freedom.

Which brings us back to the politics of *Behold the Earth Mourns*. Govinden does not call it a feminist novel, preferring to emphasize the "female-centered" character of the second part of the story and Yagesvari's "emerging female consciousness as . . . [she] decides to act in order to deal with the predicament that she is placed in."[22] To the extent that Yagesvari is a female satyagrahi, she does represent a challenge to patriarchal strains in the Gandhian tradition—which makes her, and Singh, a certain kind of liberal feminist. By making normative womanhood and the family the affective center of the novel, Singh insists that we read 1946–48 not just as a story of a racialized Indian merchant minority but also as one of social and cultural reproduction, triumphant and in crisis simultaneously. As Mongia demonstrated in her re-reading of the satyagraha campaign of 1913, it's this crisis that enables Indian political action in South Africa—its very condition of possibility—even while it has been secreted in the folds of struggle and even heritage history. If Singh's is a reclamation project, its object is primarily Srenika: the novel does not have a critical perspective on his class position but, rather, redeems his sentimental education as evidence of Indians' willingness to resist the depredations of the white racist state.[23] The Indian woman is also reclaimed through the martyrdom of Yagesvari, who, as we have seen, models the tragic possibilities of the female satyagrahi. Both she and her husband are heroic inside a certain limited framework, one circumscribed by the gender ideals of the Indian middle class: a secular Hindu formation as much as a racial one. Inside this frame, and as Govinden observes, *Behold the Earth Mourns* might be read as a "utopian" novel, redemptive of a specific strata of Indian community in South Africa and possibly even exemplary for its ongoing political development.

There's no question, then, that the novel is a species of both struggle literature and heritage history, if only with respect to the stories it tells about one segment of the Indian community in South Africa. But it is precisely this segmented reading that requires our critical energy. If we read only for Indian characters and the experiences of the Indian community—if we look only at the sightline/cite-line—Singh's novel affirms a very particular kind of anti-apartheid history: one in which second generation children of trader families are galvanized to political consciousness and action at the site of racial exclusion as Indians, utterly removed, apparently, from all contact with Africans and certainly segregated from the political activities organized for and by Africans that animated the late 1940s. These include the formation of the ANC Youth League in 1944 and forms of African militancy like mass action, boycotts, strikes and civil disobedience (known in 1950–52 as the Defiance Campaign). Written in the shadow of these developments, *Behold the Earth Mourns* gives flesh and bone to the first several generations of Indian traders who protested legislation that targeted Indians as a racialized minority. While the novel does not witness collective African activity, it does register the impact of Africans on Indians' political activities by plotting African characters centrally and purposefully at its structural heart. As we shall see, in a context when many Indians saw "kaffirs" in racially negative terms at least in part because they feared that a racist state wished to confine the two communities to a similarly subordinate and dispossessed fate,[24] *Behold the Earth Mourns* suggests how and why Indian racial and political coherence was both *made through* and *dependent on* the work, both literal and figurative, of Africans in the struggle.

Mayibuye Afrika; or How "the Earth Mourns"

Despite Srenika's conviction that his political education is self-made —a combination of internal struggle with self over family duty and internecine struggle with Krishandutt over what the best path of action with respect to racism is—the novel itself offers an alternative explanation. Immediately following his passionate manifesto about the "true spirit of non-violence" and the "cause" of physical suffering (quoted at length above), he is interrupted by Serete Luseka, an African described as "Srenika's companion for many years," who "chimed in unemotionally: 'For heaven's sake, what babble. What high level cheap bla.'"[25] Surprised to see him (Serete was "unnoticed" until his critique of the speech), Srenika "was not surprised at Serete being unmoved." This is one of several glimpses we get into their prior acquaintanceship. Serete then counters Srenika's Gandhian speech with his own:

> 'I am part of a life where it is a jungle existence for me. To live, to breathe, is the survival of the fittest from the point where conception takes place in our mother's womb. We have to thwart the elements, thwart the physical background; our home life is unstable, divided and depressed. From our early days in our cradle when we suckle our mothers' breasts, our body and our mind, our attitude has to be timid, fearful, bending and humble. When we reach an age when we can clearly reason and question, the explanations never satisfy us.'
>
> [Srenika responds]: 'Serete, when are you going to grow up? This kind of feeling is harmful to you. Your cynicism can be destructive.'
>
> 'Do you think you can turn the fear that hurts within me into a quiet suffering and expect repentance from whoever causes it? [Serete replies] Do you think you can retard and push back my personality, my rights as a human being and expect me not to suffer? Do you think our suffering is going to cure other people's evil?...'
>
> 'Yes Serete, man has a conscience and when that is awakened they then try to make amends. When this happens your children, our children will live in this beautiful country in peace and harmony, and we will be a great nation of the world in the true spirit of equality.'
>
> 'Jesus Christ—Amen,' Serete exclaimed in a manner of coldness that froze Srenika. He took the script [of Srenika's speech], pushed it into the desk and said, 'Come Srenika, it is time for us to join our friends.

I am still, more or less, one of a batch of volunteers, and will try to follow your path.[26]

This exchange captures a dimension of interracial political engagement that is rarely visible in conventional archives. However fictional, it conjures in dialogic terms some of the tensions between "Indian" political idealism and "African" realism on the ground in South Africa and especially in and around Durban, where the 1946 passive resistance campaign was centered. Critics of the novel may well say that it writes out the history of political economy from which these differences stem. Indians politicized by the events of 1946–48 were typically traders and Africans their customers, but whatever economic success they had also shut Africans out of trade, fostering misunderstandings and smoldering resentments that produced a variety of violent encounters, the most famous being the Durban riots of 1949, which took place after the time of the novel but before Singh would have written it. And of course their segregation and dispossession was orchestrated by a colonial and then a "national" state, each of which linked the fates of the two communities via a multiple racial, and racializing, governmentality, however discrepantly.[27] Singh does not deal with the macro- or micro-economics of Indian-African tension, but she does stage their ideological differences as situational rather than political: as products of history rather than as static identities per se. Serete emphasizes the structural conditions from which his "cynicism" has been borne, invoking maternal care in ways that anticipate Yagesvari's later condition even as he emphasizes the brutality of childhood and daily life for Africans. That he does so at the threshold moment of Srenika's immersion in passive resistance protest—they head off directly after this exchange into a crowd of "thousands" of demonstrators—signals how joined they are in the project at this critical, experimental, moment, even if they are speaking past one another ideologically.

When Srenika is arrested shortly thereafter, the first person he turns to is Serete; they go to jail together. They undress, shower and experience the first moments of incarceration and some hard labor together as well. "Serete," he asks, referring to the breaking of stones to which they are consigned, "is this not a waste of human energy? What on earth were crushing machines invented for?" Serete responds: "This is your punishment. This, my boy, is part of the labor sentence that makes for our spiritual and physical survival." Not only does Serete sarcastically remind him of his high talk of spiritual survival in this quip, he calls him "my boy"—a loaded term in any racialized society. Here, it signals both a reversal of the racial hierarchy of brown employer over black worker and possibly even the fatherly or avuncular political mentorship they both recognize Serete offering Srenika.[28] Because talk is forbidden between prisoners, Srenika goes into solitary as a result of this exchange. When he comes out, someone is at the gate offering to pay his fine. Knowing he will be deemed a coward if he accepts, he declines the offer—and when he next comes out on parade, Serete praises him for his courage: "the others have heard the news. We're proud."[29] Thanks to his friendship with Serete he also gets the protection of the "lifers," which proves essential to keeping him alive during his prison sentence.

What these scenes illustrate is how dependent Srenika was on Serete for his survival as well as his political education in the context of the 1946 campaign. They speak as well to an uneasy, uneven and even intermittent history of brotherhood that students of South African history will recognize from later prison accounts, Nelson Mandela's included.[30] *Behold the Earth Mourns* registers a set of reciprocal exchanges that hint at the possibilities of cross-racial cooperation (in South African terms, "non-racial") we have come to understand that the Passive Resistance movement made haltingly, fitfully possible, but for which we have very little affective evidence.[31] Most of this comes to us via Srenika, who is struck, for example, by the vastness of the crowd as well as by "every variation of the dark faces, ebony black, mahogany skinned, light brown, pallored yellow and lemon tinged olive, in their Sunday best. Some came in tailored costumes and matching hats, others in vivid saris of orange and red, emerald, yellow and sapphire blue. The eye could not miss a single color of the rainbow . . . every color was mixed with other colors and against them stood out the Satyagrahis in white."[32] But we see the promise of cross-racialism having its effect on Serete as well. When the satyagrahis are taken to their cells to await trial, Srenika among them, Serete is impressed by how orderly and unchaotic the detainees are. "That nothing could have aroused madness in their expression, that their deep-seated agony could only be poured out in their voices, that they could be poor, insecure, but could still say 'Nkosi Sikeleli Afrika' [God Bless Africa] without anger and bitterness—he would remember this happy day, for on this day the light of liberation had dawned."[33] It's important not to romanticize these episodes. For one thing, this is one of the few passages in which Serete is granted any interiority of his own, and he ratifies satyagrahis' views of themselves in a saccharine and quite uncharacteristic way, given what we know of Serete's politics. And I would maintain that the sovereign subjects of the narrative remain Srenika and Yagesvari. At the same time, Serete is neither invisible nor passive, neither a completely cardboard character nor an insubstantial one. He consolidates Srenika's political identity as a racialized subject (an identity apart, indicated by Srenika's capacity to see the white satyagrahis so starkly against the "rainbow" crowd) even as he points to the existence of some formative, because shared and cross-racial, political experiences. In this respect, Singh's novel models how racial identities may be at once shored up and unsettled in the thick of political struggle.

Serete continues to play an indispensable role in the story, and well beyond Srenika's initial political education. He comes to Srenika after prison, unable to find work and speaking of an ill wife, also out of work, and hungry children. Even Srenika, rarely observant and (at this moment in the narrative) filled with visions of his bride-to-be Yagesvari, cannot help but notice Serete's changed aspect: "shrunken with bent shoulders, drawn and tired. His skin looked dry and parched for the want of nourishment. His eyes were dark and hollowed out with sadness. Even the once large lips shriveled up and looked as if they would readily spit sarcasm, whereas it only flowed before."[34] The two reprise their earlier arguments about idealism versus the real world, about which Serete is full of despair. In response to Srenika's philosophical critique of material things he counters: "but how does all this improve my situation? How do I get a job, some money, some land to build a home. I must breathe, eat, sleep. Neither God nor the devil give me anything."[35] Srenika too has hit hard times and he employs Serete to help him with his business by suggesting "a new method to rid the overloaded firm of its goods." Is this the informal/black market? The novel is unclear. But Serete now works for the Nirvani business, and it throws them both into more regular contact, both formal and informal, including at a picnic. This is buoyant and racially mixed company—Indians, whites, Serete and a coloured four year old named Bunnie. They talk and joke quite freely, even risquély, about Srenika's betrothed and all agree she must have papers to come. The outing ends with Serete sing-saying the following song, with a prophetic ending about a doomed bride, whence the title of the novel:

> I dreamt of the valley of a thousand hills
> Whose vales had fortune of beauty and bounty
> A thousand tears shed filled the stream murmuring
> 'The winds sing thy name and behold the earth mourns.'[36]

His song invokes H.I.E. Dhlomo's epic, "Valley of a Thousand Hills," one of the staples of "native" South African literature written by a self-confessed admirer of the Indian passive resistance movement.[37]

As political guru and family prophet, it is Serete who informs the Nirvanis of the law excluding Indian brides. He brings the news to Krishandutt while Srenika is in Bombay courting Yagesvari. Serete gives Krishandutt his political education too:

> Up to now, Srenika, you or anybody else could go to any country, marry and safely live here as normal married people expect to do, but from now on you cannot do this and this means that Srenika's wife may not be allowed to live here. In fact she will not be allowed into the country...[38]

While the news of the wife ban politicizes Krishandutt as nothing else has, for Serete it is just more of the same. "Is it not natural that a man, when he marries, can live with his wife in his country? Is it not right to marry from choice? This to me is the most important protection—this freedom to choose a wife and live in one's own country. Serete, is this not so?" Serete replies: "Well yes, if you have a soul. We have not. We are not given as much consideration as even the animals get."[39] That Serete and Krishandutt bond so palpably over the blow that the wife ban deals to conjugality confirms the possibility of cross-racial brotherhood, sealing it in this instance through a shared heteronormativity that reaches across race if not class. Indeed, the proximity of class difference, here structured in part by race, is never far from the surface of the plot—a fact that underscores their interdependence but precludes any facile interpretation of cross-racial solidarity.

Serete's role is not limited to the political education and financial security of the Nirvani brothers. Once she arrives, he teaches Yagesvari to drive. By any standards this scene and the one that follows, which takes up all of chapter 20, are arguably unprecedented in the annals of South African fiction before the 1960s. On the road, Serete sings her a mournful song about colonization, diamond mines, "shacks for the brown, the coloured and the blacks," and hopes for "peace and humanity to emerge" to end the separation between races and their suffering.⁴⁰ He tries to talk her out of her despondency, and eventually takes over the wheel of the car. He invites her and Srenika to a party that night, "organized," he tells her, "to swell our charity fund." They attend but Srenika can't dance, and is not interested in learning the dance everyone is doing: The Square. Yagesvari regrets that Srenika "made it difficult sometimes."

> 'It was always one way for him,' [she thought] 'the serious way—the doing, the thinking of it all.' While she was wishing for him, Serete came back to her and swayed her towards the center of the floor gliding on the wings of a three-beat melody, and she gave herself up completely to its mellow softness.⁴¹

Evidence of this kind of social intermingling is not widely accessible in extant histories of the 1940s and 1950s though we know it did exist, often as the result of the overlap between political alliances and sociability, at least before the high noon of state-ordered banning, and even then. Though as a dance partner Yagesvari clearly yearns for Serete rather than Srenika, what's suggested here is not a sexual liaison but a meeting of the mind and spirit, in a mixed semi-public space, with bodies touching. Later, she is present when Srenika and Serete have one of their heated political discussions, again revolving around the polarity of idealism versus materialism (Serete: "the whole set up is based on economy") and despite seeing the wisdom of Serete's position, she takes her husband's part. As for the structure of the novel as a whole, these encounters are critical to the political education of Yagesvari, enabling her to inhabit the role of satyagrahi she is later to take up.

Yagesvari also has regular contact with Anna, the family maidservant. Anna helps her unpack, tries to see that she eats and looks after herself and reassures her that South Africa is in fact her home. And yet their interactions are more strained than Yagesvari's and Serete's. While she sketches Anna, they have a short, staccato conversation initiated by Yagesvari's inquiries into Anna's life. Anna tells her about her stillborn children, her troubles with her husband and the general poverty of her life at home. Yagesvari clearly doesn't know about, let alone understand, the township system or the pass laws, and declares that she wants to come visit her. "You can," says Anna, but

> 'You have to get a paper to come to the farm. The land does not belong to us.'
> 'Then who does it belong to?'
> 'That is a long story Yagesvari.'
> 'Why did your husband leave you, Anna?'
> 'This place grow big, big like this.'
> 'Keep your hands down please, Anna.'
> 'I show you all right. More chimneys come, more smoke, and more husbands leave wives.'
> 'But why did he leave you behind?'
> 'He can't bring me. He find another woman.'
> 'But why did he leave you?'
> Yagesvari was exasperated. She could not understand. Well she would try another time and went on with her drawing....[42]

The chasm of racial difference between her and Anna is apparently so stark that Yagesvari can't imagine how to assimilate Anna to her consciousness except via a "sketch." It's telling too that Yagesvari can hear the history of struggle that Anna is telling her via her account of herself, but she has no idea what it means—not in local/South African terms or in terms of the world of women either. Her class, caste and subcontinental origins partly explain the distance that difference makes here, but the scene of their failed connection is surely the most dystopic one in the book and as such, throws doubt on anything like a celebratory reading of the larger narrative. All of this leads one to conclude that the making of racially specific identities in the context of emergent non-racial politics works mainly through a fragile and uneven confraternity—a critique of both universal sisterhood and of the self-evident applicability of the idioms of brotherhood beyond the world of men. *Behold the Earth Mourns* models "solidarity" unevenly and hardly unproblematically, even as it maps the emergence of decidedly "Indian" forms of anti-apartheid politics.

Coda: Cheek by Jowl; or, Histories of "High Low In-Between"

As must be clear by now, it is not possible to apprehend the historical significance of *Behold the Earth Mourns* without attending to the twin narratives of cross-racial possibility (brown and black) and gendered racial self-making (normative brown via black) that the novel sites/cites in the context of a very specific moment in South African history. Like Serete when we first encounter him at Srenika's elbow, Africans are present but "unnoticed" in ways that challenge both our interpretive repertoire with respect to the events of 1946 and its canonicities—and our horizontal ways of reading across character and plotline rather than vertically, from top to bottom, as it were. As I have also suggested, critical re-interpretations of the novel must account for the gendered and embodied dimensions of political struggle in South Africa, where racial identity was cited through pollution complexes, endogamous conjugality and a class-specific spatial segregation. Embedding feminist readings in these histories is incredibly challenging and poses its own political risks: for even as the novel marks out some racial histories, others are eclipsed. To what end do we re-situate the conjugal histories at the heart of satyagraha movements in 1913 and 1946 if we fail to see, to cite, the anti-pass law campaign and the ANC Youth League strike, respectively, on the grid of these new narratives? Or to note that 1960 was the year of Sharpeville as well as the centenary of Indian indenture in South Africa? We await fully embodied histories of the cross-racial solidarities animating all these simultaneous movements; we await histories of what linked Indian and African women beyond the racial hierarchies of domestic service. Meanwhile, if we occlude the mass political activities of African men and women as we try to make available multiple interpretive possibilities, we miss a critical opportunity to challenge the politics of citation at the heart of even progressive narratives of anti-apartheid.

This is not to say that the novel's characters are without a one-dimensionality of their own. Srenika is very much the peace-loving Indian, Serete the "violence-prone African"—both direct echoes of some of Gandhi's own writings about the violent proclivities of Africans and of longstanding tropes in other iterations of South African history.[43] Even if Srenika recognizes Serete's condition, it is arguably presented in a "social work" discourse with eugenic dimensions.[44] In a very real sense, *Behold the Earth Mourns* is a Gandhian novel, if we recognize that Gandhi's attitudes towards Africans were not just complex, but racialist as well. In the context of both South African history and Indian diaspora history, this may be the most challenging interpretation of all. Beyond Gandhi, we need methods for seeing and reading Indians' racialized identities which both concede the stereotypes and challenge easy readings about what they mean, for whom and at what specific historical junctures.[45] We need methods for reading the citationary apparatus of anti-apartheid politics in all its racial complexity, and all its gendered and sexualized historicity.

Given the 150th anniversary of indentured Indians' arrival in South Africa in 2010, will 21st century audiences in South Africa and/or beyond be interested in Singh's novel? Much depends, I think, on how it is cited. In an era of global history, transnational literary criticism and diaspora studies it makes sense, as Govinden does, to situate Singh's novel in all of those frames—but only if those frames, in turn, do not (however unwittingly) read out the interracial intimacies, collisions and encounters that it has archived. *Behold the Earth Mourns* certainly belongs in the company of Indian "national" literature, whether global or diasporic, and it can profitably be compared with texts by black South African men and women as well. Yet as a citationary practice, both of these moves raise questions about the elasticity of the categories "national" and "black" respectively, and of course, interdependently, since postcolonial Indianness writ large was also forged in relation to Africanness in the context of Cold War Afro-Asian "solidarity." For if and when such comparative frames disappear Serete and Anna and their contrapuntal role in the plot, they are in danger of marginalizing Singh's work, even ghettoizing it, in new and politically problematic ways—in part because they can retread the purportedly discrepant histories of Indians and Africans, in part because they can occlude the historical and contemporary political power of race, with all its multiple axes and its densely embodied genealogies.

I want to at least register the possibility that the so-called hidden histories of cross-racial politics in the novel have been "hidden," out of sight, below the footnote line, because they are unremarkable: because readers simply recognized the mixed racial world it represents and didn't think anything of it. Ironically, the convergence of its sesquecentenary with both the arrival of the World Cup in Durban and the celebrations of the sesquicentenary—phenomena which produced their own crisis of Indian-African relations on the ground, in terms of the politics of political economy, of market gardens and international capital, of Zuma governmentality and local histories —may throw the interracial politics of *Behold the Earth Mourns* back into bold relief.[46] It should also illuminate the perils of even an interracial reading of the kind I have done here: for despite the novel's dedication "To South Africa on the centenary of the arrival of Indians in the country," laboring Indians—coolies, laboring people—make virtually no appearance in the text. For a certain class of South African Indians, then, it was apparently easier to cite and to read Africans at the heart of the struggle than working-class Indians: a reminder, in turn, of how vexed the collective, "community" identity of Indian settlement in South Africa was, as well as how multi-axial *our* critical readings need to be to capture the full historicity of a novel like *Behold the Earth Mourns*.[47]

To read Singh's novel in the history that is now, I think, means acknowledging that it cannot be confined to the precincts of heritage history; it must be cited in a wider set of domains. *Behold the Earth Mourns* shares ground with Gillian Slovo's *Every Secret Thing*, the 1997 memoir of her mother Ruth First's life, death and political romances at the heart of interracial South African politics in the second half of the 20th century (subtitle: *My Family, My Country*). Hence, of course, my interrogative at the start of this essay.[48] As a kind of political memoir *Behold the Earth Mourns* could also be read alongside or against Mamphela Ramphele's *Across Boundaries*, where Indians, and Indian-African connections, erupt briefly in her account of the struggle—or, for that matter, alongside any number of accounts of prison life in the 1950s and 1960s now being generated at an accelerating rate.[49] And because of the way it displays the tripartite verticalities of white, black and brown, it merits a place on the shelf right next to Imraan Coovadia's 2009 novel *High Low In-Between*, where African servants are a fascinating plot device, puncturing the haughtiness and uneasy aspiration of Indians in the new South Africa.[50] That few struggle texts, whether heritage or not, visualize Indian coolies in any sustained way is surely consequential to what continues to be read out of South African history *tout court*. What is clear is that conjugality—as a matter of affect and law, and in all its colors—is central to each of these aforementioned narratives, reminding us (as if we could forget) of how relentlessly embodied histories of interracial politics and struggle have historically been, and of course remain.

I take the question of juxtaposition, of proximity, seriously because literature and politics belong together, though not self-evidently and, I would submit, often in unlooked for and promiscuous ways. In that jointness they may help to interrupt the reproduction of racial narratives that "artificially partition South Africa's complicated and tangled past"—a possibility that the "150 years" celebrations certainly have the capacity to realize.[51] However it is canonized, and even were it not, if a 21st century return to *Behold the Earth Mourns* stimulates a new, and renewable, set of axes of comparison, it just might continue to spin anti-apartheid histories on new and as yet unimaginable pivots, as all critical histories exhibit the capacity to do.

Notes

1 Shabbir Banoobhai, *Echoes of My Other Self* (Johannesburg: Ravan Press, 1980), p. 36.

2 I am indebted to Sarah Ahmed's *Queer Phenomenology* (Duke, 2006) for this formulation.

3 In South African parlance the term is "nonracial," meaning "irrespective of race." Because that meaning may not be totally clear to other readers, in this chapter I use the term "cross-racial" and "interracial" to describe activities or encounters between Indians and Africans. In doing so I realize that I risk fixing racial difference and distance, though that is not my intention. For a detailed and thoughtful account of the origins of the term see Jon Soske's review of David Everatt, *The Origins of Non-Racialism: White Opposition to Apartheid in the 1950s* (Johannesburg: Witwatersrand University Press, 2009), forthcoming in *Transformation*. Crucially, Soske argues that "individual ANC leaders seem to have adopted the language of non-racialism after the organization's banning and reactively. It did not develop organically out of the debates over race and party structure of the 1950s." For "non-European," a contemporary if not a cognate term, See Uma Mesthrie, "Indian Responses in Natal to Non-European Unity Moves, 1927 to 1945," *Journal of Natal and Zulu History*. 12 (1989): 73–89.

4 For an excellent textual and pictorial introduction to these questions see Uma Dhupelia-Mesthrie, *From Cane Fields to Freedom: A Chronicle of Indian South African Life* (Cape Town: Kwela Books, 2000). For earlier takes see Fatima Meer, *Portraits of South African Indians* (Durban: Avon House, 1969); B. Pachai, *The International Aspects of the South African Indian Question, 1860–1971* (Cape Town: C. Struik, 1971); and T.G. Ramamurthi, *Apartheid and*

Indian South Africans: A Study of the Role of Ethnic Indians in the Struggle against Apartheid in South Africa (New Delhi: Reliance Publishing, 1995).

5   See Goolam Vahed, "The Making of 'Indianness': Indian Politics in South Africa During the 1930s and 1940s," *Journal of Natal and Zulu History* 17 (1997): 1–36; Mesthrie, "Indian Responses in Natal to Non-European Unity Moves, pp. 73–89; and Jon Soske, "Navigating Difference: Gender, Miscegenation and Indian Domestic Space in Twentieth-Century Durban," in Pamila Gupta, Isabel Hofmeyr and Michael Pearson, eds., *Eyes Across the Water—Navigating the Indian Ocean* (Pretoria: Unisa Press, 2010), pp. 197–219.

6   Ansuyah R. Singh, *Behold the Earth Mourns* (Cape Town: Cape Times Limited, 1960). The inside jacket describes it as "the first novel by a South African Indian." For a repetition of this claim see Bernth Lindfors, *African Textualities: Texts, Pre-Texts and Contexts of African Literature* (Africa World Press, 1997), pp. 29–38; and Devarakshanam Govinden, *Sister Outsiders: The Representation of Identity and Difference in Selected Writing by South African Indian Women* (Pretoria: Unisa Press, 2008), pp. 143–172. Singh is also listed as a part of the "New African Movement (1900–1960)": see http://pzacad. pitzer.edu/NAM/newafrre/writers/singh.shtml, last accessed March 2011.

7   Govinden, *Sister Outsiders*, p. 171. Singh's is not one of the texts recovered in M.J. Daymond et al., *Women Writing Africa: The Southern Region* (New York: Feminist Press, 2003).

8   Toni Morrison, *Playing in the Dark: Whiteness and the Literary Imagination* (New York: Vintage, 1993).

9   See E.S. Reddy, "Indian Passive Resistance in South Africa, 1946–1948," http://www.anc.org.za/ancdocs/history/congress/passive.html; originally from *Mainstream*, New Delhi, April 5, 1997.

10 See Enuga Reddy and Fatima Meer, eds., *Passive Resistance 1946: A Selection of Documents* (Durban: Madiba Press, 1996), p. 19.

11 Singh, *Behold*, p. 2.

12 *Ibid.*, pp. 6 and 7.

13 *Ibid.*, p. 10.

14 Surendra Bhana and Goolam Vahed, *The Making of a Political Reformer: Gandhi in South Africa, 1893–1914* (New Delhi: Manohar, 2005).

15 K.G. Naidoo, *Coolie Doctor* (Durban: Madiba Press, 1991/Hyderabad: Orient

Longman, 1998). For an extended treatment of autobiography see Antoinette Burton, "The Pain of Racism in the Making of a 'Coolie Doctor,'" *Interventions: International Journal of Postcolonial Studies* 13, 2 (2011).

16 Singh, *Behold*, pp. 16–17.

17 Gayatri Spivak, "The Rani of Sirmur," *History and Theory* 24, 3 (1985): 247–272 and Lata Mani, *Contentious Traditions: The Debate on Sati in Colonial India* (Berkeley; University of California, 1998).

18 Bhana and Vahed, *The Making of a Political Reformer*, especially chapter 5.

19 Radhika Mongia, "Gender and the Historiography of Gandhian Satyagraha in South Africa," *Gender and History* 18, 1 (2006): 132 and ff.

20 See "List of Passive Resisters" and "Members of the Joint Passive Resistance Council of Natal and Transvaal," in Reddy and Meer, eds., *Passive Resistance 1946: A Selection of Documents*, p. 394.

21 J.H. Abramson, Ansuyah R. Singh and Victoria Mbambo, "Antenatal Stress and the Baby's Development," [received for publication June, 1960], *Archives of the Disease Childhood* 36 (1961) 42–49. For a concise biography of Singh, including details of her working life, see E.J. Verwey, ed., *New Dictionary of South African Biography* (Pretoria: HSRC Publishers, 1995), pp. 226–27.

22 Singh, *Behold*, pp. 156–7.

23 As Isabel Hofmeyr observes, "If the novel parallels 1913 and 1946, then one major shift between these two events has been the status of the diaspora (to use contemporary terminology). In 1913, South African Indians held high symbolic prestige and represented a version of India itself. By 1946, the indentured diaspora had lost much of its value. In 1913 India was imagined in imperial terms, as a dominion within empire, a situation in which the diaspora acquires some cache. By 1946, as the nation became more anti-imperial, it became more national. In this context, the diaspora loses value. Indeed by 1946, the diaspora in Africa had become something of a political embarrassment: Nehru definitely wanted them to stay put and certainly not think of coming 'home.'" Email communication, January 18, 2010.

24 See for example Heather Hughes, "'The Coolies will Elbow us Out of the Country,'" *Labour History Review* 72, 2 (2007).

25 The spelling shifts between Srete and Serete across the course of the novel in the edition I worked with; I regularize it as Serete here to minimize confusion.

26 Singh, *Behold*, pp. 17–18.

27 I draw here from Renisa Mawani, *Colonial Proximities: Crossracial Encounters and Juridical Truths in British Columbia, 1871–1921* (Vancouver: UBC Press, 2009), p. 76.

28 This is an interesting counterpoint to Gandhi's prison memoirs, which are preoccupied with shoring up racial boundaries. See David Arnold, "The Self and the Cell: Indian Prison Narratives as Life Histories," in Arnold and Stuart H. Blackburn, eds., *Telling Lives in India: Biography, Autobiography and Life History* (Bloomington: Indiana University Press, 2004), pp. 29–53.

29 Singh, *Behold*, p. 29.

30 Nelson Mandela, *Long Walk to Freedom* (Boston: Little Brown, 1994).

31 For a full account of this fitful process see Jon Soske's brilliant dissertation, "'Wash Me Black Again': African Nationalism, the Indian Diaspora, and Kwa-Zulu Natal, 1944–1960," doctoral thesis, University of Toronto, 2009, provided generously by the author.

32 Singh, *Behold*, p. 18.

33 *Ibid.*, p. 19.

34 *Ibid.*, p. 25.

35 *Ibid.*, p. 67.

36 *Ibid.*, p. 75.

37 See Ursula A. Barnett, *A Vision of Order: A Study of Black South African Literature in English* (London: Sinclair Brown, 1983), pp. 12–13. Ismail Meer claims in his autobiography to have been present at the creation of the poem, when he and Dhlomo were together in the Valley. See Ismail Meer, *A Fortunate Man* (Cape Town: Zebra, 2002), pp. 121–22. One leading black scholar of African literature, B.W. Vilakazi, did not think highly of the poem "because it failed to pass from the region of the sensuous to the higher realm of interpretation of life" (Barnett, *Vision of Order*, p. 252).

38 Singh, *Behold*, p. 85–86.

39 *Ibid.*, p. 87.

40 *Ibid.*, p. 129.

41 *Ibid.*, p. 133.

42 *Ibid.*, p. 145.

43 "Men who see far believe that the problems which are connected with the Natives will be the problems of the future, and that, doubtless, the white man will have a stern struggle to maintain his ascendancy in South Africa. When the moment of collision comes, if, instead of the old ways of massacre, *assegai* and fire, the Natives adopt the policy of Passive Resistance, it will be a grand change for the Colony..." Quoted in "Dr. Yusuf Dadoo, Mahatma Gandhi and the South African Struggle," and published in *Mainstream*, New Delhi, September 16, 1989, and *Sechaba*, November 1989. The quote is attributed to Joseph J. Doke, *M. K. Gandhi: an Indian Patriot in South Africa* (1909). See http://www.anc.org.za/ancdocs/history/people/gandhi/8.html.

44 Thanks to Isabel Hofmeyr for helping me think through these possibilities.

45 This raises questions as well about the shifting meaning of homeland and diaspora and the politics of Indian "location" as well.

46 See http://www.streetnet.org.za/wccacampaignnews.htm (World Class Cities for All); http://www.ukzn.ac.za/ccs/default.asp?2,68,3,1890 (Center for Civil Society, UKZN); and Caroline Skinner, "The Struggle for the Streets: Processes of Exclusion and Inclusion of Street Traders in Durban, South Africa," *Development Southern Africa* 25, 2 (2008): 227–42.

47 I am grateful to Sukanya Banerjee for helping me to appreciate this point. For one of the best readings of this question in relation to Gandhi in South Africa see her *Becoming Imperial Citizens: Indians in the Late-Victorian Empire* (Durham: Duke University Press, 2010), chapter 2.

48 Gillian Slovo, *Every Secret Thing: My Family, My Country* (Boston: Little Brown, 1997).

49 Mamphela Ramphele, *Across Boundaries: The Journey of a South African Woman Leader* (Feminist Press, 1995); Robert D. Vasssen, ed., *Letters from Robben Island: A Selection of Ahmed Kathrada's Prison Correspondence, 1964–1989* (East Lansing: Michigan State University Press, 1999) and Mac Maharaj, ed., *Reflections in Prison* (Amherst: University of Massachusetts Press, 2001).

50 Imraan Coovadia, *High Low In-Between* (Cape Town: Umuzi, 2009). I am indebted to T.J. Tallie for helping me acquire, and then think through, this novel.

51 See Omar Badsha and Jon Soske, "150 Anniversary: Anxieties of Commemoration—Towards a National Dialogue," April 18, 2010 : http://historymatters.co.za/ [A Blog Promoting Citizenship and Democracy in South Africa].

Chapter 2

Race and the Politics of Position
Above and Below in Frank Moraes' *The Importance of Being Black* (1965)

From now on, nobody can look down on Africa.
Kwame Nkrumah, April 1958, Accra[1]

Time and again I found myself comparing Asia and Africa.
Frank Moraes, *The Importance of Being Black*

"'I grant you that some African top leaders are capable men,' remarked a white settler at Lusaka in Northern Rhodesia. 'But what's below them? Nothing but scum and scoundrels.'"[2] Thus opens Frank Moraes' book, *The Importance of Being Black*, published by Macmillan in London and New York in 1965. Very much the view from an airplane (he never lived in Africa), it is nonetheless a critical ethnography of emergent African nation-states—refracting the fate of postcolonial India and Indians through its telescopic lens and honing in on African practices on the ground as evidence (or not) of Africans' fitness for self-rule. As this anecdote suggests, "above and below" operate in several registers across the landscape of his 400+ page account, offering a decidedly, if complexly, vertical challenge to claims about the horizontal, south-south political solidarity that was presumed to cross-hatch the postcolonial "Third" world in the wake of the 1955 Afro-Asian solidarity conference in Bandung. Moraes' promontory view was refracted through a variety of civilizational, racial and gendered hierarchies that unsettled his would-be flyover perspective, in ways he acknowledged and in ways he did not. This essay plays with the scalar complexities of his citationary maneuvers in an attempt to provide a more nuanced history of what remained of the imperial "below" in the 1960s and in order to capture some of the cultural dimensions of the post-imperial Afro-Asian "solidarity" that is a largely unremarked feature of the geopolitical terrain of the Cold War.

Frank Moraes (1907–74) was a Goa-born editor for the *Times of India* and worked for a number of other newspapers during his career as a journalist. The author of numerous books on a variety of Cold War subjects, including one on Mao's China and two studies of Nehru, he wrote only this book on Africa, which is an account of his travels there in 1960.[3] The continental aspiration of the book is worth lingering on, for it establishes Africa as a very particular kind of ground, a very specific species of referent, from the first pages. That ground—the "below" as seen from the airplane window—is ostensibly highly differentiated, with each chapter mapping the history and contemporary politics of emergent nation states from Ghana to Rhodesia to Kenya to the Congo. "Flying from the Arabian peninsula across the Gulf of Aden to Djibouti in French Somaliland," Moraes writes in the chapter 3 (entitled "The Lion of Judah"),

> where we changed into a gaudily painted Convair of the Ethiopian Airlines, the landscape was flat and arid. But over the plateau of Ethiopia the scenery grew more varied—green and untamed, with here and there a dry riverbed and long narrow trails snaking their way over the hillsides. Through the vaporing clouds one saw little sign of habitation and life until suddenly below us, spread on a brilliantly verdant carpet, was Addis Abbaba.[4]

In the most literal sense, Moraes' approach to many places in Africa is from a high altitude; he continually touches down, landing readers in the middle of a fraught Cold War political situation or a deep, tangled and intermittently verdant anti-colonial history—or both. The rhetorical effect of this touch-down strategy is twofold. First, it registers "Africa" not simply as an undifferentiated geographical mass but as a fitfully decolonizing space under pressure from mass nationalist movements and superpower competition. What appears to be specificity from above turns out to be—agonistically, in Moraes' rendition—repetitively familiar when seen from the ground: decolonization in crisis, with differences of degree rather than kind across a variety of newly postcolonial states. Second, it allows Moraes to claim a particular form of postcolonial knowledge: deep and drilled-down, in so far he disembarks into a series of local communities, but shaped by an overall conviction about the condition of the continent as a whole that assimilates small differences to an again familiar trope of failed-ness in process. His chapter-by-chapter catalogue of emergent states enables him to claim knowledge about the specific genealogies of the present, effectively credentializing him as a specialist with both a continental view *and* local knowledge in the service of a larger continental authority. It codes him, in other words, as the quintessential cold war expert, with the view from 60,000 feet (with access to the technology that guarantees it) and the purposefully angled vision of a participant observer as well.

The seduction of this simultaneity—of the collapse of above and below in the service of information, knowledge and power—is not new to the 1960s but, is of course, an inheritance of the colonial surveillance state, however imperfect we concede its capabilities to have been. What's significant here is how readily Moraes, as a self-identified "Asian"/"Indian" observer of postcolonial African politics, follows in its wake. The subtitle of the book orients us immediately—for this is *The Importance of Being Black: An Asian Looks at Africa.* Taken as a whole, that look, that regard, is directed outward, from the platform of an almost 20 year old independent India down onto a nascent, even adolescent, quasi-independent Africa-in the-making. A quote:

> The average African truly certainly lacks the education, training and experience not only of the European. but of the Asian. If he is a hundred years behind Europe, he is at least fifty years behind Asia in the development of his aptitude and abilities.

Here the ground that Africa occupies is multiply "below": underneath not just Europe, but Asia as well. Nor is the bildungsroman of African development vis a vis Asia only implicit. As Moraes remarks as early as the second page of the text,

> the feeling of an adolescent Africa as against a comparatively adult Asia ... lingered and haunted me throughout my stay there. It seemed as if Africa bristled with very many angry young men. Like children they felt afraid to walk alone in the dark, but at the same time they were resentful and suspicious of anyone who might light their way.[5]

As the subtitle of the book suggests, a major structural feature of the narrative is Moraes' viewpoint as an Indian observer, looking down not simply from his vantage point as an individual but from the promontory view of a nation that has already accomplished what Africa seeks to achieve. If India is the presumptive leader of Asia, it is also the metaphorical equivalent of the airplane. Moraes articulates not just a promontory view but a technological "above" with an underdeveloped below in ways that establish hierarchies of brown over black and position Africa as subordinate to India in geopolitical terms as well.

More specifically, *The Importance of Being Black* presents a series of political diagnoses from the vantage point of a representative of the comparatively new Nehruvian state, which saw itself in turn as a patron of emerging African nations: as *prima inter pares* in the context of Afro-Asian confraternity. "To an Indian," he observes, "Africa offers a study of parallels."[6] Moraes peppers his narrative with examples of such parallels: comparisons that typically place African states in a position of tutelage, an object of pedagogy in the primer of Gandhian/ Nehruvian state-making. So, African universities are impressive, but not comparable to Indian ones; the gap between urban and rural is wider in Africa than in India; citizens in newly independent African states are as disoriented now as Indians were 20 years ago; Africa is passing through the same "phase" India did just after independence; and, somewhat ruefully, "like the British in India, the British in Africa, as well as the French, unconsciously taught the Africans to revolt against them."[7] In this scenario, the account from "below" Moraes promises to provide is more than the story of the creation of postcolonial polities from the bottom up. In an echo of earlier colonial stagiest discourse, "below" in Moraes' "Africa" also means behind: in capacity, in time, in development per se—a domain that includes politics, economics and the social as well. He repeatedly suggests that if Africa in the 20th century has been called to the sightline of modernity in terms of its negative relationship to a certain First World universalism—serving as a kind of foundational referent, a globally acknowledged touchstone from which it must ascend in order to be recognized as a legitimate participant in the promise of global modernity—it also passed (and continues to pass) through a series of hierarchical relationships internal to the Third World through "acts of relegation," strategies of foregrounding and backgrounding, that produce Africa as a dependent of Asia and of India within it.[8] Via his ethnography in *The Importance of Being Black*, Moraes is both a witness to this process and an agent of its discursive violence.

To what extent were such acts of relegation articulated out of superstructural remnants of British imperial power? Despite Moraes' stated interest in contemporary African politics, he is preoccupied with the impact of the Raj, which he sees as a template for the end stage of colonialism in Africa. The book is brimming with references to how western attitudes towards Africa now mirror British views about India before 1947.[9] This preoccupation impacts his view of African capacity: he quotes Sir Philip Mitchell, former British governor of Kenya and Uganda: "[Africans] . . . are a people who in 1890 were in a more primitive condition than anything of which there is a record in pre-Roman Britain."[10] It's not just that the Raj provides Moraes with a framework for the verticality of imperial power or for the deep civilizational bottom that Africa historically represented. It's that the British empire's core-periphery binary is the lens through which he apprehends the worlds of postcolonial Africa as well. Though Accra may be civilized and sophisticated, he tells readers, the village of Aburi just 25 miles out one finds

> crowds of half-naked, hysterical tribesmen [who] screeched war cries and . . . chiefs, brandishing their hatchets or swords, swayed as the drums beat and the horns blared. One had the feeling of being in the Africa of Rider Haggard.[11]

In places, as above, his references are literary. In others they identify with a very long historical, and very broadly anglo-saxon, imperial hubris, as when Moraes remarks that Verwoerd "can no more contain the tide of African nationalism in South Africa than King Canute could stay the waves." As tellingly, the geographical signposts of British imperialism also shape his representations of formerly French or Belgian territories: "if Katanga was the Ruhr of the Congo, it was also its Ulster." And lest there be any doubt, Moraes concludes that "the benefits of colonialism, however incidental or accidental, cannot be denied."[12] Elsewhere, Moraes acknowledges that Africans he met were "particularly allergic to the Asians' unvoiced but undisguised feeling of cultural superiority"—referring presumably to Indian settlers in Africa while describing his own promontory view to a tee.[13]

Moraes' citations of the imperial past may have seemed analogically useful in his postcolonial present, but they imposed a restrictive frame on both his argument and his capacity to see beyond an immediate pre-postimperial history. At least one of his contemporaries, the noted linguist Suniti Kumar Chatterji, shared his preoccupation with the relationship between India and Africa but traced it to a far more distant past. His 1968 book, *India and Ethiopia From the Seventh Century BC*, cites deep and longstanding links between these two ancient civilizations, anticipating later historiographies of ocean world contact and drawing on a variety of sources, from classic Arabic manuscripts to analyses of loan-words to the first edition of Richard Burton's *First Footsteps in East Africa*.[14] Chatterji's interest was piqued by his trip to Addis Ababa in 1966, which was sponsored by the Education Ministry of the Government of India: a reverse flow of the kind of institutional Africa-India traffic that was the subject of Chanakya Sen's novel, *The Morning After*, dealt with in the next chapter. But Chatterji was equally inspired by the work of his colleague Harit Krishna Deb, whose interest in the "history of racial and other movements in ancient times" dated from at least the 1940s, and who with Chatterji's encouragement wrote a paper on the subject for the *Journal of the Asiatic Society* in 1948. That paper, which helped to date the final version of the *Satapatha-Brahmana* because of its references to 7th century BC Egyptian potentates, was, significantly, not well received by fellow Indian scholars. By Chatterji's account, they responded "with reserve" and "not . . . sympathetically."[15] This resistance did not daunt Chatterji. He set about his own researches, focusing as much on Abyssinia as on Egypt per se. "I read whatever I could lay my hands upon regarding the history of the entire region as one unit—Egypt, Nubia and Abyssinia or Ethiopia." These included works by Sylvia and Richard Pankhurst as well as one scholar, Abraham Demos, at the University of Addis Ababa.[16]

Chatterji's book is a sweeping history, taking us all the way to the 1960s. He pays particular attention to the Habshis, those "Abyssinians or Ethiopians"—elites, slaves and eunuchs—who found their way to

India from the 12th century onward. They "carved out for themselves a little state on the Bombay coast," Janjira, in the 16th century which came under direct British rule in 1870, only to be "merged" into Indian in 1948. "'Habshi' people are now found in western areas of India," Chatterji explains, "and they retain their separate social existence and remnants of their mongrel speeches—Somali, Gala and Arabic."[17] Tellingly, Chatterji was keen to see his work cited as a contribution to Afro-Asian solidarity as well as to ancient history and linguistics. His book was dedicated "to the memory of the Indian merchants and sailors, and Indian teachers, who linked up India with the World of Ethiopia, during the last two thousand years." That dedication also included reference to Indian soldiers "who made the Supreme Sacrifice on the Soil of Ethiopia for the Freedom of the Ethiopian People"—an allusion to the work that Indian soldiers, engineers and laborers did in 1936–41 as part of the British imperial army's support for Haile Selassie I.[18] There is a trace in Chatterji of the above and below so characteristic of Moraes' work, though it might be considered more of a cultural promontory than a racial one per se. "I have to place on record my high admiration of the way in which Ethiopians are progressing," he concluded in the foreword to his book. "Already we have a number of Indian nationals helping Ethiopia in her reconstruction and rehabilitation in a spirit of brotherly cooperation; and it is in this same spirit that this little book is placed as an offering at the shrine of Indo-Ethiopian Friendship and Mutual Service."[19]

Chatterji's scholarly work took him around the world in the course of his career at the University of Calcutta and as a member of the West Bengal Legislative Council. He went to Africa in 1954 on a trip arranged by the Indian Council for Cultural Relations (Delhi) and by Nehru himself. While there he met Nkrumah, which makes him an early ambassador of Afro-Asian solidarity.[20] In his 1960 book *Africanism: The African Personality*—written just at the time of Moraes' own African tour—Chatterji confesses to his own racial prejudice. "Like most people in India and elsewhere, I used to think the Negroes of Africa were a savage and barbarous people and they had nothing of civilisation and art, of thought and religion of any high order, comparable with what we find among civilized people."[21] Even as he attributes his own transformation to his encounters with both Africans and African art in postwar London as a student, he leaves no doubt as to where he thinks India ranks in that ladder of civilization, a position partly enabled by the African example, if only implicitly so.

It is tempting to chalk up Moraes' preoccupation with above and below to anglophilia and to link it to the larger phenomenon of cultural continuity between the Raj's last masters and their successors in the Nehruvian state, of which there is ample historical evidence even if postcolonial historians themselves have been slow to amass and analyze it.[22] The case of Chatterji enables us to appreciate Moraes' views not as idiosyncratically racialist, or even representative of a "collective outlook," but rather as part of the broader question of the making of the Indian self—in this case, in a postcolonial mode that evidences more continuity than break with earlier notions of civilizational ordering and its correlative, racialized citation.[23] Indeed, the ideological work of positioning Africa below India that Moraes does here was enabled as much by the racial and civilizational hierarchies between Africa and India that were a staple of 19th century British imperial policy and discourse. At the highest levels of decision-making, British expansion in Africa, though prompted by a variety of local, regional and international factors, was justified in Whitehall by virtue of the jewel-in-the-crown argument: India and the routes to it must be secured for the sake of national/imperial security. Though I am perforce compressing a very complex set of histories here, that premise was born of convictions—ethnographic, linguistic, religious and sociological—about a kind of racial chain of being which posited Aryans at the top and Africans at the bottom, with inhabitants of India closer to the former by virtue of a variety of "familial" connections that were, in turn, but expressly and allusively racial. As Tony Ballantyne has shown, the transnational imperial reach of Aryanism as a marker of civilizational difference was enabled in part by the racialized and racializing hierarchies, of color and of capacity, it carried.[24] Nor was this relevant to the making of only Indian postcolonial identities. As the career of Dadabhai Naoroji, and particularly of his ambition to be a member of parliament at Westminster in the late Victorian period, colorfully illustrates, Indian subjects seeking imperial citizenship had to prove their distance from blackness as well as their overall fitness for such a "right" in the admittedly polycultural, often porous but nonetheless vigorously vertical world of imperial power.[25]

Moraes slips rather effortlessly into this vertical racial framework more than half a century after Naoroji's bid, positioning Indians as in-between white Europeans and black Africans in ways that reproduce colonial lines on a postcolonial grid. Indeed, as the book's subtitle indicates, this liminal space is the position from which he looks down on Africa itself. To be sure, when superimposed on Africa from above, the older binary—India is to Britain as Kenya is to Britain or the Congo is to Belgium—makes for an uneasy fit with the realities he encounters below, on the ground, in the places he visits. These include evidence of tangible gains on a variety of fronts, including education, agricultural development and parliamentary government. Moraes cannot but be impressed by some of the "progress" he observes as well as by the strongmen—Jomo Kenyatta, Kwame Nkrumah, Julius Nyerere—whose nationalist programs he chronicles. Nor he is an uncomplicated racist. African "backwardness," he assures his readers, "is not the result of anything intrinsically inferior in the African's mental make up, but of the deliberate denial to him of opportunity for development.[26] Even allowing for Moraes' racialized views of the postcolonial Third World, he is close enough in historical time to look empathically, if not paternalistically, on Ghanaians and Kenyans struggling to exceed the constraints of long and deep colonial pasts and build new societies. We might call this posture a cross-racial fraternity, where cross-racial signifies not the erasure of difference but a recognition of its explanatory power. We might even call it a recognition of the currency of negritude in a Cold War, if not a postcolonial world. This interpretation is particularly germane for Moraes' take on Nkrumah, whose emphasis on the African personality Moraes reads as a rallying cry across internal divisions and indigenous verticalities: a way of co-opting "the angry young men" of the continent into a workable program of uplift and development. He calls this "the Pan-African cult" and compares Nkrumah to Hitler, arguing that he "preaches a contrary chauvinism based on the importance of being black."²⁷

Jomo Kenyatta expressly rejected the association of Africanism with "chauvinistic nationalism and economic autarky" both in *Facing Mount Kenya* and in a variety of public speeches and writings.²⁸ Nkrumah, for his part, famously believed that "salvation for Africa lies in unity." He also acknowledged that India's model for independence—"steady evolution"—was effective, but took over a quarter of a century to accomplish.²⁹ Moraes is torn between a grudging admiration for the cultural capital of blackness and an acute awareness of how Indian settlers in various quarters of the continent are subject to what, in his scheme, amounts to a reversal of the racialized hierarchies of brown over black bequeathed to Indians by British colonialism. Of particular note is Nyerere's frank position: "Asians are welcome . . . as long as they contribute to Tanganyika's progress. We are in no need of traders and moneylenders. But we want technicians, managerial talent and sound investors with a stake in the country's prosperity."³⁰ Significantly, Nyerere did not dispute the impact of Gandhi and Indian independence on his own anti-colonial development.³¹ And as Jon Soske has shown, African intellectuals in general looked to 1947 and India both as a kind of "historical mirror, a device that allowed them to reflect on Africa's colonial experience and future prospects."³² But here Nyerere is clear: he wants not just the plane Moraes rode in on but the capacity to design, manage and own the whole fleet—and he wants Indians who can contribute to that kind of project with Tanganyikan success in mind. In chapter 12, Moraes calls this an "East African tangle," and he reads the Ismaili community as a palimpsest, if an uneasy one, for the "problem" of Indians in Africa more generally.[33]

Given when Moraes was touring Africa, it is hardly surprising how preoccupied he was with "the Asian problem." He spends considerable space dilating on the numbers, which he estimated at 900,000, and mapped their differential presence across the continent. Though he dwells on it only briefly in the book, his travel notes suggest his connections with the Indian trading company Chellaram, which had interests, and markets, in Nigeria.[34] Most significantly, Moraes anticipates that as African nationalism in its negritude iterations accelerates, "in all likelihood the Asian, rather than the European, will be the first commercial casualty"—both because they are competitors for employment and hold themselves "separate . . . and aloof" from Africans.[35] The Ismailis were the exception; following the lead of the Aga Khan, they "seemed closer to the Africans than the Indians, realizing their lot was with the Africans and not in between." In a rare direct quote from any Indians in Africa, Moraes reported that the South Asians he spoke to in Dar-es-Salaam—whether "Indian" or "Pakistani"—were keenly aware of the internal, cross-racial hierarchies of above and below to which they were subject at this particular, precarious moment in East African history. He cited them as saying: "Africanization is bound to affect us . . . Nyerere is reasonable and far-sighted. But who's below him? The extremists. Sooner or later he will have to sing their tune."[36] In Moraes' account, then, Indian settlers sing the same tune as the white settler from Lusaka who opens his book (and this essay). By the time he gets to Kenya, Moraes is parroting the line of the likes of Charles Markham, a white Kenyan, who tells him that after Mau Mau, "the Asian is as much up against it as the European." Though he admits Markham was "a European extremist," he labels those Africans who agreed with Markham "moderates." One such was Musa Ambalemba, then minister for housing. Predictably, Moraes likens him approvingly to Tej Bahadur Sapru, "an Indian liberal ... who was a cautious, farseeing patriot in the ebullient heyday of the Congress party."[37]

There is obviously much more that could be said about the impact of the Indian settler on Moraes' take on "the importance of being black." At the time of his continental tour, Indians in East Africa were already on the road to their shift from being "a privileged to an unwanted minority."[38] Just over a decade later Prem Bhatia would write that

> we in India have often taken a sentimental and unrealistic view of relations with Africa. As the political and economic underdog of a colonial past, the African has usually commanded our sympathy and invariably our political support. Our expectations of reciprocity included hope of a fair deal for Indian settlers. Disappointment in this regard amounts for many to a shock over unrequited love. The shock became deeper after Amin's savagery in Uganda. Conversely, we have sometimes unfairly put all the blame on the Indian settler for the unkind treatment he has received ... a new arrogance has begun to shape the conduct of the Africans.[39]

One effect of the Indian settler predicament is to compel Moraes into elaborating a recurrent set of asymmetrical links between Indians and Africans around tribe and caste that *appears* to produce grounds for comparison, via a putative equivalence, but which ends up re-iterating the view from above that, in the end, characterizes the whole book. "I had heard much about tribalism while I was in Africa from both European and Asian acquaintances, he writes, "and the Congo as well as Kenya have highlighted this basic organization of the African way of life."

Yet sometimes as an Indian I could not help thinking that our own caste-conscious society, riven by linguistic and local divisions, also represented a form of tribalism, though perhaps of a more sophisticated order. Another parallel obtruded. In India, as in Africa, tribalism or divisiveness has kept spilling over when the lid of foreign domination, was lifted.[40]

Africa is, he continued,

> a giant with one foot in the primitive past and another in the twentieth century. India also has disparate layers of culture, from the highly sophisticated to the aboriginal, but the latter represents a microscopic miniscule. In India too, there prevails a strong sense of diversiveness induced by its medley of castes and languages, and by the factionalism bred of provincial feelings. But Africa's divisiveness crisscrosses the entre continent, and expresses itself in innumerable tribes, and in about a thousand languages and tribal dialects ... [in contrast[]] India's constitution recognizes fourteen principal languages, including English, and India has a population nearly double that of Africa.[41]

Still farther along, he compares the panchayat and the tribal council, whose similarities as "institutional forms of democracy" struck him "forcefully".[42] That these nodes of comparison have no ethnic or linguistic specificity signals is, I think, a process of erasure that makes the lesson about cross-racial affinity possible. The two places are similar, but not in filial terms; they are parallel but distinct; and at almost every turn, the connective tissue that begins the comparison is undone by evidence that privileges India. So caste is similar to tribalism, but "of a more sophisticated order;" India also has "disparate layers of culture" but only microscopically so; India has diversiveness, Africa divisiveness that "crisscrosses the entire continent." And in the end, India is the baseline referent, the a priori sign, and Africa the signifier: for it is Swahili "that might be described as the Hindustani of Africa," and not the reverse.[43]

Moraes participates in, and re-articulates, a long history of what Ania Loomba calls a "colonial and Indian exceptionalism" that "has insisted that caste is sui generis, that it cannot be compared to other discourses of difference because it is quintessentially and uniquely Indian"[44]—and he does so resolutely in the service of shoring up a postcolonial nationalist Indian identity rooted in racial difference as much as in racial particularity per se. Here, comparison functions as a claim to identity through racial differentiation between non-white formations—formations still laden to some degree by imperial categories but promising the possibility of some kind of shared "native" democratic forms as well. As Loomba has also observed, race and caste are "highly malleable categories which have historically been deployed to reinforce existing social hierarchies and create new ones." And indeed, while Moraes' comparison between caste and tribe yields one of the most potentially progressive moments in *The Importance of Being Black*, it is fleeting. Or, rather, the domain of parallel/equivalent indigenous political practice it hints at is not borne out anywhere else in the text, which emphasizes Asia's solidarity with the West versus Africa's marginality from it—a "fact" with historical genealogies that, Moraes' argues, negritude only exacerbates, to Africa's detriment.[45] This, combined with "the African's extrovert exuberance, fortifies the foreign belief that a certain untamed wildness characterizes him." Though he expresses confidence that it will recede with time, Moraes insists that this "sense of differentness assails a European and, frankly, even an Asian in the presence of an African."[46]

Who was Moraes' audience for all this, one might ask? The book was published in both New York and London and was clearly aimed at a western readership, even perhaps a diplomatic one; indeed, by his own confession, the quality and character of the Afro-Asian relationship was paramount in a world context.[47] And that global context was structured by a pincer movement that was both vertical and horizontal: the US-USSR superpower grid. "Unless Africa itself fills the vacuum from which it has emerged," Moraes wrote, "it must inevitably be the stepping ground of the two power blocs."[48] If this was a new kind of "below" for Africa, it certainly had implications for India as well—to which as Nehru's non-alignment policy, with its Afro-Asian presumptions, was a testament. *Foreign Affairs* published an essay by the exact same title (and subtitle) of Moraes' book in 1964, on the threshold of its release in New York and London.[49] The essay version is arguably sharper, less cluttered by the travelogue mannerisms that beset the book. But it's also more polemical, rehearsing all the major planks of Moraes' arguments about Africa in a tighter, less expository frame. An exemplary line might be this one: "While all the utterances in all parts of the world are conditioned by the circumstances in which they are made, in Africa the conditioning is not controlled. It stems from a habit of mental indiscipline born of the colonial hangover, of uncontrolled ambition and of the triple continental course—poverty, ignorance and disease."[50] Africa and Asia, tribe and panchayat, remained paired, and Indian emerges the "cosmopolitan" society as against Africa's comparative chaos. The central question in Moraes' *Foreign Affairs* piece is not comparison per se but rather: "is authoritarian government essential for rapid economic growth in a society with precarious political moorings?"[51] In response to this question, Japan emerges as the model in contrast to India, with the latter's slow economic growth chalked up by over-planning and "over-nationalization."[52] If he critiqued African chauvinism, Moraes always did so with a dose of anti-communist rhetoric, in the essay and in the book both—not because he believed anti-colonial nationalism and communism were inextricably tied, but because he believed that "color, not creed" would prove the deciding variable, even as he claimed to lament that it might be so.[53] "Africa and Asia, he wrote at the very start of his book, "are still conscious of the bond of color, as the overworked term 'Afro-Asian' implies."[54]

Readers in the US found Moraes' views alternately surprising, distasteful and unnecessarily censorious. Writing for the *New York Times Book Review* in 1965, Roland Oliver—who was to become the don of African studies in Britain—lamented the excessively political focus of the book, wishing Moraes had given more "vignettes of life outside the capital cities."⁵⁵ He was not alone in comparing Moraes to the American Cold War journalist and commentator John Gunther, whose "Inside" books combined a kind of continental grand tour approach with contemporary sociological and political commentary. Gunther's 1955 *Inside Africa* may have been on reviewers' minds when they picked up *The Importance of Being Black* and found it wanting.⁵⁶ Oliver, for his part, was frankly shocked by what he called Moraes' style of "white south African polemics," citing the "half-naked, hysterical tribesmen" quote with the quip: "one almost expects him to go on . . . to say that these people never invented the wheel."⁵⁷ In his view, Moraes' patent lack of sympathy for Africa undercut the force of his political observation. C.L. Sulzberger, Foreign Affairs columnist for the *New York Times*, acknowledged some valuable aspects but was otherwise negative, calling the book "wordy" and a "jumble" and lamenting that much of what Moraes had written about "changeable" Africa was already out of date.⁵⁸ In contrast to Oliver, Sulzberger echoed Moraes' racial views rather than critiqued them, citing with approval his attention to the "difficulties of Asian minorities today . . . in a continent vibrating with the pride of new independence and the savagery of released racial hatreds." And puncturing the simple hierarchies of white v. black, Sulzberger reproduces Moraes' view that "the extremes of white man and black man . . . tend to engulf the reluctant brown man as well."⁵⁹

Though the London *Times* reviewed nearly all of Moraes' other books it does not appear to have noted *The Importance of Being Black*. The same seems to be true for the *Times of India* and if African newspapers covered the book, I am not aware of it. Sulzberger's review for the *New York Times*, meanwhile, featured a photo of a group of unnamed, African men (the caption is "Accra, Ghana") who looked to be gathered for a rally or a demonstration, and his headline was "Hotter Heads Prevail." Needless to say, the world of postcolonial Cold War diplomacy was a homosocial one—underwritten by various forms of imperial, colonial and anti-colonial forms of brotherhood—and only a very few women broke into it, at great peril to their own reputations for respectability, let alone credibility when it came to high politics and international affairs.[60] The verticalities of gender generally ran in one direction and they were well nigh impossible to re-orient. Significantly, though none of his reviewers remarked on it, Moraes did engage the question of women, however briefly. And unsurprisingly, given what we know about how entangled gender and sexuality are in racial thinking and its idioms, he comes closest to what we might call classic imperial racial language—with the complex aboves and belows they entail—when he talks in *The Importance of Being Black* about African women. Discussions of women's emancipation are thin on the ground in his text, despite the way they shaped nationalist discourses in anti-imperial movements, as the work of Susan Geiger and Jean Allman has so brilliantly shown.[61] Possibly because he seeks company almost exclusively with elite postcolonial African men, Moraes rarely encounters politicized African women; one exception is a group of Nyasa women, being addressed by Vera Chirwa, who was connected to the Malawi Congress party. He deems them, glancingly, "a most colorful assembly."[62] Women rarely puncture the published narrative and when they do, it is in stereotypical terms, as in the "living ebony Nefertiti with supple elongated neck and high, idealistically molded cheekbones" he sees in the streets of Accra.[63] Significantly, the diary he kept while on his African tour is much more sexually explicit, recording in quite lascivious terms the bodies of African women he encountered in the course of his travels and often focusing completely unself-consciously on the size of their breasts and bottoms.[64] The dedication of the book ("for Marilyn, who observed far more than I saw") is intriguing at a minimum, because his diary makes no mention of her.

Marilyn was Marilyn Silverstone, a London-born photojournalist with Magnum who met Moraes, then the editor of the Indian Express, in India in the 1950s.[65] They were together until his death in 1974. Moraes' marriage to Beryl Moraes was troubled from the 1940s onward, in part it seems because of her mental illness, which their son the poet Dom Moraes recounts with great poignancy in *My Son's Father: An Autobiography*.[66] If Frank Moraes had any sexual encounters with African women during his "grand tour," they are not recorded. This may have had to do with Marilyn's presence, or with the very real pollution complexes that, rhetorics of Afro-Asian solidarity notwithstanding, undergirded Indians' apprehensions of relationships with Africans on the ground in the newly postcolonial world across which Moraes moved. Or both. Reminiscing about him in her memoir, *Portraits of an Era*, Tara Ali Baig commented on Moraes' capacity to keep work and emotional life separate: in his book, *Witness to an Era*, she observed, he gave " a lively account of Burma and the War" but left no trace of "the war that took place in his own heart and mind"—i.e., the impact of his peripatetic life and acquaintances on his marriage and on his wife's sanity.[67] Baig recounts his encounter with the photographer Margaret-Bourke White as "electrifying" and as a catalyst for his own realization that "he was changed, and [that] he had to admit that to himself and to Beryl."[68] Of the "personal tragedy" of Beryl's mental illness and his role in it he, apparently, rarely spoke of even to friends. So that if Moraes had sexual encounters in Africa without recording them even in the diary, we might chalk it up to this now life-long professional separation of spheres.

Given the racial context, we may also be dealing with a form of shame and self-loathing around miscegenation—the miscegenation of looking as well as of "doing"—that we have very little historiography for in any time and place, let alone this one. Regardless, the simultaneous occlusion and pathologization of African women in Moraes' writing reflects the ways in which *The Importance of Being Black* depends, rhetorically and ideologically, on a racial confraternity that is fragile in part because it cannot exceed the hierarchies embedded by centuries of colonial rule, in part because even the sodalities of Bandung are routed through its strictures and prohibitions—the prohibitions of interracial sexuality included. The confraternity that Moraes reaches uneasily for via his standpoint as an Asian/Indian looking down on Africa is always already compromised because it is based at once on the legacy of the Raj's subimperial status vis a vis Africa *and* on the unstable and arguably fictive discourse of Afro-Asian solidarity whose hyphen signals parallel rather than comfortably entwine histories between black and brown. How and whether this uneasy confraternity entailed homosocial intercourse of various kinds is a hugely important arena of research that is, needless to say, crying out to be fully historicized.

When I gave a version of this paper in Britain in summer of 2010, one listener raged at "my" suggestion that Nkrumah was comparable to Hitler and all but called Moraes a racist. When I gave another iteration in Delhi in winter 2011, some observers distanced themselves from Moraes' racial views by suggesting that as a Goan, he was not Indian—implying that this technicality of birth made the Indian-African connection and its politics of citation moot. Though the racial taxonomies of Goans in an Indian Ocean world context is surely an important marker of Moraes' positionality, it is not a pretext for distancing his brand of "Africanism" from Indian postcolonial identity per se.[69] Others at the Delhi paper proffered the view that Moraes was right, that Africans were below Indians in the 1960s and were clearly in need of technological uplift from the Nehruvian state. One audience member drew parallels between this kind of patronage and Indian technocratic aid to poor countries in Southeast Asia in the last half-century.[70] If the airplane view—in all its verticalities and with all its disidentifications—persists, it was not unique to Moraes now or then. Even as late as the mid-1960s, very few observers could exceed these different but historically related—and of course, culturally produced—traces of imperial governmentality of the vertical kind we see in *The Importance of Being Black*. The view from the airplane to which I have referred was no less critical to how Africa *qua* Africa was apprehended in this extended postcolonial moment. European access was frequently, if not exclusively, virtual, as British Pathe films that literally swoop down on Kenya to showcase the atrocities of Mau Mau bring powerfully home.[71] And one has only to think of Nelson Mandela recalling the impact of his own airplane view of the subcontinent—in disguise, as he fled the long arm of the apartheid state—in the early 1960s to appreciate not just the complexity of views from above but the role of the airplane itself as a continentalizing technology, for Africans as well as Europeans.[72]

As Mandela's contemporary Robert F. Kennedy said in his famous Day of Affirmation Speech in South Africa in 1966:

> In a few hours, the plane that brought me to this country crossed over oceans and countries, which have been a crucible of human history. In minutes we traced migrations of men over thousands of years; seconds, the briefest glimpse, and we passed battlefields on which millions of men once struggled and died. We could see no national boundaries, no vast gulfs or high walls dividing people from people; only nature and the works of man—homes and factories and farms—everywhere reflecting man's common effort to enrich his life. Everywhere new technology and communications bring men and nations closer together, the concerns of one inevitably become the concerns of all. And our new closeness is stripping away the false masks, the illusion of differences which is at the root of injustice and hate and war. Only earthbound man still clings to the dark and poisoning superstition that his world is bounded by the nearest hill, his universe ends at river's shore, his common humanity is enclosed in the tight circle of those who share his town or his views and the color of his skin.[73]

Such liberal American universalist idealism stands in stark contrast to the preoccupations with racial difference and racial particularity on offer in Moraes' text—though the backdrop for it is of course US civil rights unrest and violence, which was to prove an all-consuming fire on the ground for RFK. Nor could anyone listening to that speech with a memory of Mau Mau fail to know, or to remember, how firepower was used and how vividly airstrips and airports and "flying boats" figured in the imagination—brown, black and white—of that time.[74] And it's frankly hard not to hear the drone of those airplane engines as they roar overhead, descend to deliver the alien witness and stand by to collect "African" knowledge gathered by yet another continental traveler/ethnographer/extracter. It's hard as well to resist rematerializing not just Moraes and his gaze but the transformation of technological development—in all its competitively racialized postcolonial complexity—into a new kind of civilizational superiority that the view from the airplane now affords for some privileged "Asians."[75]

Whereas Gandhi had the train car for shaping his apprehensions of (South) Africa and its racial politics, then, Moraes had the airplane: a difference of degree rather than kind even if the platforms they offered produce discrete views out of the proverbial window.[76] Yet —and this is worth noting—Indians did not need either an airplane or the triumph of independence to prompt an aerial view of Africa. Here is Benarasidas Chaturvedi, hero of the Greater India movement:

> It is said that some of our Indian Sadhus in olden times had a sort of a miraculous power by which they could fly away to any part of the world. I wish some Sadhu like that could send a good number of our leaders to the colonies in a twinkling of an eye. Let them be sent to Mombasa and Dar-es-Salam. Let them see that Mombasa is just like another town of Gujurat. Sir John Kirk, the British agent at Zanzibar, used to refer to East Africa as India's America. Let some of our leaders see this America.[77]

In this analogy, America is to India what Africa was to the British: supine and ready for flyover, touchdown and settlement. As such, it poses an interesting challenge to recent readings of Afro-Dalit solidarity between the US and India reminding us of how historically specific grids of connection perforce are—and how complex the relationship between citationary practices across time can be. For his part, when Moraes concluded that "you never see Africa whole until you are out of it,"[78] he was hardly the only contemporary to do so. Indeed, I would contend that to the extent that Indian postcolonial theory has engaged the question of Afro-Asian solidarity, it too has retained the view from 60,000 feet inherited from the Olympian vantage point of Bandung and after, presuming that the hyphen signals equal ground rather than a complex of histories in dynamic and often violent tension, with very real consequences for postcolonial history-writing and contemporary south-south alliance building.

This is what Maria Todorova, in her essay on balkanism and postcolonialism, calls "the beauty of the airplane view." It's a view whose beauty, she says, lies not simply or only in the eye of the beholder, but precisely in the angle of the historian's eye—and, in our case in the kinds of superimpositions that are made available by that optic in, and across, particular historical times.[79] In a set of exchanges with Dipesh Chakrabarty on the stakes of provincializing Europe and as significantly, in the context of an argument about the need to give race its proper place in South Asian histories, Amitav Ghosh recently observed that "the truth is that India was to the late 19th century what Africa was to the 18th—a huge pool of expendable labour."[80] In Ghosh we hear not a reversal of Moraes' work but a specific chain of logic that appears to be readily available for comparisons that position India on the same level as Africa, though unevenly and unenviably so even from a 21st century Indian's point of view. This is to say nothing of the labor "Africa" has done, and continues to do, in the postcolonial imagination, Indian and otherwise. If, in conjunction with Moraes' Africa book, V.S. Naipaul comes to mind—both his 1979 novel, *A Bend in the River*, and his 2010 travelogue, *The Masque of Africa*—the association raises questions about postcoloniality less as an identity than as a historical condition which Indians of a variety of political persuasions have in common, and in which Africa figures variously if vertically with respect to the new nation and/in the world.[81] To echo J.M. Coetzee, Moraes' Africa was out of Rider Haggard while Naipaul's was out of Conrad; though both writers are temporally postcolonial, they remain remarkably late-Victorian in many ways.[82] Can Hugh Trevor-Roper, with his infamous claims in 1963 about the "gyrations of barbarous tribes," be far behind?[83]

The overlap of post/colonial temporalities warrants neither surprise nor lament. It requires, instead, sustained attention to the durability of colonial tropes in the context of postcolonial sovereignty, and to their familiar points of reference: what Grant Farred calls the exigency of "reflexive historical encounter" and what we might call a reflexive account of the politics of citation.[84] Moraes, for his part, shares much with, and indeed presages, contemporary postcolonial critique where questions of race and especially blackness are concerned, not least because that critique itself bears the imprint of verticalities—of politics and imagination—produced by empire and the various "belows" it set into motion, collision and competition well into its long, persistent and ineluctable afterlife.

Notes

1 Quoted in Frank Moraes, *The Importance of Being Black: An Asian Looks at Africa* (New York: Macmillan/London: Collier-Macmillan, Ltd., 1965), p. 34. All subsequent references to the book are to this edition.

2 Moraes, *The Importance*, p. 1.

3 He did not go to South Africa, having been denied a visa, though he wrote a chapter about it nonetheless.

4 Moraes, *The Importance*, p. 42.

5 *Ibid.*, pp. 2–3.

6 *Ibid.*, p. 93.

7   *Ibid.*, pp. 9, 2, 24 and 35.

8   Sarah Ahmed, *Queer Phenomenology: Orientations, Objects, Others* (Duke 2006), p. 31.

9   Moraes, *The Importance*, p. 29.

10 *Ibid.*, p. 32.

11 *Ibid.*, p. 9.

12 Moraes, *The Importance*, pp. 368, 211, 34.

13 Frank Mores, *Witness to an Era: India 1920 to the Present Day* (London: Weidenfeld and Nicholson, 1973), p. 265. Neither his *Introduction to India* [with Robert Stimson] (Oxford: Oxford University Press, 1945) nor his *India Today* (New York: Macmillan, 1960) makes reference to Africa at all, in contrast.

14 Suniti Kumar Chatterji, *India and Ethiopia from the Seventh Century B.C.* (Calcutta: The Asiatic Society, 1968), pp. 21–22. For a less positive view of pre-colonial connections and relations see Dhruba Gupta, "Indian Perceptions of Africa," *South Asia Research* 11, 2 (1991): 158–61.

15 Chatterji, *India and Ethiopia*, p. vii.

16 *Ibid.*, p. vii.

17 *Ibid.*, p. 66.

18 For footage of this campaign see British Pathe's "Ethiopian Campaign 1941," http://www.britishpathe.com/record.php?id=84885; accessed March 2011.

19 Chatterji, *India and Ethiopia*, p. ix.

20 Sukumari Bhattacharji et al., eds., *Suniti Kumar Chatterji: The Scholar and the Man* (Calcutta: Jijnasa, 1970), pp. 20–21. He was also president of the India-China Friendship Society in Calcutta "but he resigned from this office at the Chinese aggression of India in 1961" (p. 13).

21 Suniti Kumar Chatterji, *Africanism: The African Personality* (Calcutta: Bengal Publishers Private, Ltd., 1960), p. 76. One study of Chatterji's thought suggested that the book was motivated by "one very important question —whether the old African culture can survive in the modern world." See Surajit Dasgupta, *In Quest of World-Culture: Suniti Kumar Chatterji* (Calcutta: Shankar Prakashan, 1977), p. 59. Several commemorative volumes ignore his African work altogether: Bhakti P. Mallik, ed., *Suniti Kumar Chatterji*

Commemoration Volume (Calcutta: Palit, 1981) and Udaya Narayana Singh and Shivarama Padikal, eds., *Suniti Kumar Chatterji: A Centenary Tribute* (New Delhi: Sahitya Akademi, 1997).

22 A notable exception is Srirupa Roy, *Beyond Belief: India and the Politics of Postcolonial Nationalism* (Durham: Duke University Press, 2007).

23 See Gupta, "Indian Perceptions of Africa," pp. 158–74. And, pace Tagore's Nikhil in *The Home and the World*, speaking of his rival Sandip: "Had he been born in the wilds of Africa he would have spent a glorious time inventing argument after argument to prove that cannibalism is the best means of promoting true communion between man and man." Cited in Elleke Boehmer, "Without the West: 1990s Southern African and Indian Women Writers—A Conversation?" *African Studies* 58,2 (1999): 157.

24 Tony Ballantyne, *Orientalism and Race* (London: Palgrave, 2002).

25 Antoinette Burton, "Tongues Untied: Lord Salisbury's 'Black Man' and the Boundaries of Imperial Democracy," *Comparative Studies in Society and History* (2000) 43, 2: 632–59.

26 Moraes, *The Importance*, p. 31.

27 *Ibid.*, p. 124.

28 Jomo Kenyatta, *Suffering without Bitterness: The Founding of the Kenyan Nation* (Nairobi: East African Publishing House, 1968), p. 227.

29 Kwame Nkrumah, *Africa Must Unite* (New York: International Publishers, 1963), pp. 145 and 53.

30 Moraes, *The Importance*, p. 256.

31 "The significance of India's independence movement was that it shook the British Empire. When Gandhi succeeded I think it made the British lose the will to cling to empire. But it was events in Ghana in 1949 that fundamentally changed my attitude. When Kwame Nkrumah was released from prison this produced a transformation. I was in Britain and oh you could see it in the Ghanaians! They became different human beings, different from all the rest of us! This thing of freedom began growing inside all of us. First India in 1947, then Ghana in 1949. Ghana became independent six years later. Under the influence of these events, while at university in Britain, I made up my mind to be a full-time political activist when I went back home. I intended to work for three years and then launch into politics." See the "Heart of Africa: Interview with Julius Nyerere on Anti-Colonialism," *New Internationalist*

Magazine, 309 (January-February 1999): http://www.oneworld.org/ni/issue309/anticol.htm. Last accessed July 27, 2010.

32 As Soske also suggests, "the mode of writing in these essays sometimes approached allegory: they used India to reframe the particularities of South Africa's experience within a universal history of colonial rapacity and (implicitly) post-colonial deliverance." Soske, "'Wash Me Black Again': African Nationalism, the Indian Diaspora, and Kwa-Zulu Natal, 1944–1960," pp. 112–13. University of Toronto doctoral thesis, 2009, provided courtesy of the author.

33 Moraes, *The Importance*, p. 256.

34 Moraes, *The Importance*, pp. 35–36; see also Frank Moraes, Africa Diary. School of Oriental and African Studies, PP MS 24, Box 1 v. 1 Africa 1960, file 7, September 27th, p. 100.

35 Moraes, *The Importance*, p. 36.

36 *Ibid.*, pp. 255–56.

37 Moraes, *The Importance*, pp. 295–96.

38 For a history of settler patterns and some discussion of African-Indian tensions in East Africa (especially around transport issues) see Robert G. Gregory, *South Asians in East Africa: An Economic and Social History, 1890–1980* (Boulder: Westview, 1993). Quote is from Brij Maharaj, "From a Privileged to an Unwanted Minority: The Asian Diaspora in Africa," in Philippe Gervais-Lambony, Frederic Landy and Sophie Oldfield, eds., *Reconfiguring Identities and Building Territories in India and South Africa* (New Delhi: Manohar, 2005), pp. 117–37.

39 Prem Bhatia, *Indian Ordeal in Africa* (Delhi: Vikas Publishing House, 1973), p. vi.

40 Moraes, *The Importance*, p. 5.

41 *Ibid.*, p. 25.

42 *Ibid.*, p. 396. For a contemporary echo of this see Amartya Sen quoting Nelson Mandela's account of tribal democracy in Sen's *The Argumentative Indian: Writings on Indian History, Culture and Identity* (New York: Farrar, Straus and Giroux, 2005), p. 31.

43 Moraes, *Importance*, p. 25.

44 Ania Loomba, "Race and the Possibilities of Comparative Critique," p. 14; draft manuscript courtesy of the author.

45 Moraes, *The Importance*, p. 391.

46 *Ibid.*, p. 393.

47 *Ibid.*, p. 2.

48 *Ibid.*, p. 20.

49 Frank Moraes, "The Importance of Being Black: An Asian Looks at Africa," *Foreign Affairs* 43, 1 (1964): 99–111.

50 *Ibid.*, p. 102.

51 *Ibid.*, p. 107.

52 Ibid.

53 *Ibid.*, p. 111.

54 *Ibid.*, p. 3.

55 Roland Oliver, "Being Black," *The New York Review of Books*, February 11, 1965.

56 John Gunther, *Inside Africa* (New York: Harper, 1955).

57 Oliver, "Being Black."

58 C.L. Sulzberger, "Hotter Heads Prevail," *New York Times*, January 24, 1965, p. BR 3. This was a charge Moraes directly anticipated; see Moraes, *The Importance*, "Foreword," n.p.

59 Sulzberger, "Hotter Heads," BR 3.

60 One exception in this period is Santha Rama Rau, whose public life as a writer and translator of India to the US I have tracked in *The Postcolonial Careers of Santha Rama Rau* (Durham: Duke University Press, 2007). See also Robert Dean, *Imperial Brotherhood: Gender and the Making of Cold War Foreign Policy* (Amherst: University of Massachusetts Press, 2003).

61 Jean Allman, "The Disappearing of Hannah Kudjoe: Nationalism, Feminism, and the Tyrannies of History," *Journal of Women's History* 21, 3 (2009) and Susan Geiger, *TANU Women: Gender and Culture in the Making of Tanganyikan Nationalism, 1955–1965* (London: Heinemann, 1997).

62 Moraes, *The Importance*, p. 336. See also his brief attention to women in the Sudan, *The Importance*, p. 64.

63 Moraes, *The Importance*, p. 9.

64 In Nigeria, September 24, 1960: "Women here have <u>enormous behinds</u> (underscoring his) though the faces of some—I saw one black beauty at Challaram's whose face might have been carved out of chaste ebony. She wore a sullen arrogant look." In Lagos, October 4, 1960: "Heard a row with a woman screaming. Though uninhibited sexually they are not as gay and cheerful as most negroes." In Dahomey, October 8, 1960: "For the first time in Africa saw women with exposed, elongated breasts." Frank Moraes, Africa Diary. School of Oriental and African Studies, PP MS 24, Box 1 v. 1 Africa 1960, 14 September–22 October.

65 Douglas Martin, "Marilyn Silverstone, 70, Dies; Photographer and Buddhist Nun," *New York Times*, October 4, 1999. She took her vows after Moraes' death.

66 See Dom Moraes, *A Variety of Absences: The Collected Memories of Dom Moraes* (New Delhi: Penguin Books India, 2003).

67 "I hate desk work. I like to be moving and, of course, I love people. That's really my hobby." Quoted in "Moraes Lived Close to Scene of Action," *Times of India* May 5, 1974, p. 5.

68 See Tara Ali Baig, *Portraits of an Era* (New Delhi: Roli Books, 1988), pp. 58–63.

69 For an interesting take on this see Rochelle Pinto's account of Aquino Furtado's 1928 travelogue, *Cidades Africanas*, "Race and Imperial Loss: Accounts of East Africa in Goa," *South African History Journal* 57 (2007): 82–92.

70 Jean Allman has suggested links between *The Importance of Being Black* and Richard Wright's *Black Power*, published in 1954, several years ahead of Moraes' trip. *Black Power* is text in which Wright asks hard questions about biology and culture heuristically, questions that represent Wright's sense of disidentification as well. "I had understood nothing. I was black and they were black, but my blackness did not help me." See Cornel West, ed., *Black Power: Three Books from Exile* (New York: Harper Perennial, 2008).

71 See http://www.britishpathe.com/record.php?id=49596. Thanks to Danielle Kinsey for bringing this to my attention.

72 Nelson Mandela, *Long Walk to Freedom* (Boston: Little Brown, 1994), pp. 289 and following (this was 1962).

73 http://www.jfklibrary.org/Historical+Resources/Archives/Reference+Desk/Speeches/RFK/Day+of+Affirmation+Address+News+Release+Page+2.htm

74 "Pilot Proves Good his Idea for Airstrip on Top of a Hill: Base against Terrorists", *East African Standard*, January 1, 1954, p. 7; "Air Strike Moves Gang into Open: Six Killed," *East African Standard*, January 17, 1954, p. 5; "Mr. Head Flies Over Operational Areas," *RAF Standard*, January 18, 1954. I am indebted to Zack Poppel for these references.

75 For a philosophical take on this see Martin Heidegger, "The Question Concerning Technology," http://www.wright.edu/cola/Dept/PHL/Class/P.Internet/PITexts/QCT.html. I am indebted to Zack Poppel for bringing this to my attention and encouraging me to think of the energy of the airplane and/as "standing reserve."

76 Thanks to Alan Lester for this insight. Starker still is the contrast of both train and plane views with that from the railing of the boats that brought so many indentured laborers to Africa from South Asia. See Allen De Souza, "Bombay," in Tejpal Ajji and Jon Soske, *South-South: Interruptions and Encounters* (Barnicke Gallery, Toronto, 2009), pp. 31–39. As the essay dramatizes, the shift from boat to plane could happen in one (fantastical) lifetime.

77 Cited in Gupta, "Indian Perceptions," p. 162. Original is B.A. Ogot and J.A. Kiernan, eds., *Zamani: A Survey of East African History* (Nairobi, 1973), pp. 262–63.

78 Moraes, *The Importance*, p. 23.

79 She also calls it a middle view or "velocity," neither that of a train nor of a rocket either. See her "Balkanism and Postcolonialism, or On the Beauty of the Airplane View," in Costica Bradatan and Serguei Alex. Oushakine, eds., *In Marx's Shadow: Knowledge, Power and Intellectuals in Eastern Europe and Russia* (Lanham, MD: Rowman and Littlefield, 2010), especially p. 189.

80 Amitav Ghosh and Dipesh Chakrabarty, "A Correspondence on Provincializing Europe," *Radical History Review* 83 (2002): 160. I am grateful to Ania Loomba for reminding me more than once to return to this essay.

81 V.S. Naipaul, *A Bend in The River* (New York: Alfred Knopf, 1979) and *The Masque of Africa: Glimpses of African Belief* (also Knopf, 2010). Both the novel and the travelogue derive from Naipaul's time in East Africa in 1966, around the same time Moraes published *The Importance of Being Black*.

The likeness between Moraes and Naipaul extends to Naipaul's own fragile marriage; see Paul Theroux, "Life and Letters: The Enigma of Friendship," *The New Yorker* (August 3, 1988): p. 44 and ff. For a deft analysis of Naipaul and Africa see John Thieme, *The Web of Tradition: Uses of Allusion in V.S. Naipaul's Fiction* (Sydney: Dangaroo Press, 1987), pp. 163–91 (chapter called "Darkest Conrad").

82 J.M. Coetzee, "The Razor's Edge," in Amitava Kumar, ed., *The Humor and the Pity: Essays on V.S. Naipaul* (New Delhi: Buffalo Books, 2002), p. 128.

83 Cited in A.J. R. Russell-Wood, "African History: Unrewarding Gyrations or New Perspectives on the Historian's Craft," *The History Teacher* 17, 2 (1984): 247. The Trevor-Roper quote is from his essay, "The Rise of Christian Europe," *The Listener* LXX 1809 (November 28, 1963): 871–75.

84 Grant Farred, "The Unsettler," *South Atlantic Quarterly* 107, 4 (2008): 807.

CHAPTER 3

FICTIONS OF POSTCOLONIAL DEVELOPMENT

Race, Intimacy and Afro-Asian Solidarity in Chanakya Sen's *The Morning After* (1973)[1]

A selective brotherhood is a selfish partnership.
Mohandas K. Gandhi, 1932[2]

If testimonies of African students studying in various city institutes are anything to go by, it was never easy to be "black" in Delhi.
Times of India, 2006[3]

Histories of Indian postcolonial development—by which I mean the assemblage of scientific and technological modernization programs undertaken by the Nehruvian state in the 1950s and 1960s—rarely plot nation-building projects on the grid of Afro-Asian solidarity, even though that concept was arguably the watchword of a newly independent India in the first two decades after 1947. When scholars do cite the transnationality of early postcolonial development schemes, they tend to turn back to continuities with British colonial initiatives and to think forward to American Cold War interventions in order to make the case for India's integration into the global marketplace and against what Manu Goswami calls the "methodological nationalism" haunting histories of modern India.[4] In fact, India's postcolonial developmentalist identity was intimately bound up with the Nehruvian state's "outreach" to African leaders and their constituencies in both rhetorical and practical terms. Chanakya Sen's 1973 novel *The Morning After* dramatizes one of the most important transnational postcolonial projects launched by the Indian state under the aegis of Afro-Asian solidarity: the African university students scheme. At the center of the story is Solomon Kuchiro, a Ugandan would-be poet who is attending a university in Delhi and is invited to spend some time living in the home of Shukdev Sharma, an Indian civil servant, his wife, Sulochana and their college-age children, Sheila and Romesh.[5] Although fictional, Solomon and his mentor/friend, the Kenyan Peter Kabaku, represent the cohort of African students who came to India to seek education-for-uplift through the offices of the Nehruvian government—those who lived this high-minded experiment in Afro-Asian solidarity, mingling with Indians in classrooms and residence halls, on buses and in marketplaces, in formal and casual settings. These two African men are drafted into the geopolitical re-education camp that is India, becoming students not just of the Nehruvian social and economic experiment but of its racial and sexual protocols as well. Over the course of the narrative, first published in Bengali in 1960 as *Rajpath, Janpath* (*King's Way, Queen's Way*), Solomon and Peter discover themselves as Africans in new and unsettling ways. As we shall see, their encounters in the postcolonial contact zone of Delhi and village India reveal fissures in the romance of racialism undergirding Afro-Asian solidarity and mark the imaginative limits of Indian cosmopolitanism and its developmentalist logics.

In this essay I read *The Morning After* as a postcolonial bildungsroman: a novel of Indian national development not simply built on presumptions about African underdevelopment but rooted in anxieties about the interracial intimacies that Afro-Asian solidarity in practice might entail. As with the colonial bildungsroman, about which Jed Esty has written so eloquently, the "suggestive relationship between colonialism and adolescence" is at the heart of this novel, embodied in and by various relationships between African men and Indian women.[6] In an echo and a remake of its generic forbears, *The Morning After* positions India as a new nation and a young, enterprising force on the world stage. It plays, in other words, on the global ambition that Nehru had for "Asia and Africa," a pairing that featured in his writing and thinking well before the 1955 conference at Bandung and which imagined independent India as a leader of proto-postcolonial African states in the post-imperial world. Although he denied having "designs" on any peoples and often couched Indian nationalist ambition in a larger "Asian" framework, Nehru also repeatedly cited the Afro-Asian nexus, articulating his conviction that India had a responsibility to Africa which, as he observed in 1950, "is still more or less a colonial continent."[7] India's geopolitical commitments proceeded from that lag-time framework well into the 1960s, operating on a vertical rather than a horizontal developmental axis: one which positioned the global south and emergent African nations within it as clients of Indian technological expertise and the cultural/civilizational improvement that ostensibly came with it.

The temporality of development was and is obviously crucial here; India was ahead and Africa, behind on the time-line of postcolonial modernity. As we shall see, the collision of the newly secular urban Hindu elite with the objects of Nehruvian reform—here, African students making themselves at home in the capital city and environs—disrupted the certainties of postcolonial Indian bourgeois cosmopolitan aspiration and impacted the direction of rural "community" development as well. And perhaps unsurprisingly, the densest, and tensest, transfer point in this modernizing pedagogical experiment was the domain of sexuality, with the plotline of interracial sex serving as a carrier of the political and economic valences of Afro-Asian solidarities—and conflicts—of all kinds. Nothing less than the reproduction of a specifically Indian postcolonial modernity

—in sexual, social and technological terms—was at stake. In *The Morning After* we see with particular vividness how and why the modernizing universal subject of the Indian nation was in fact a culturally particularistic and highly gendered postcolonial Indian self, reliant on the double consciousness of racial superiority (brown over black) and its correlative, sexual purity (fear of miscegenation) in the context of in/resurgent Third World politics. When development meets Afro-Asian solidarity at the heart of postcolonial India itself, the struggle over the structural terms of modernity is an intimate one, routed through a highly racialized politics of citation: structured via a geopolitical imaginary of signifier and signified, it is about who, in effect, should be on top.

* * *

Spearheaded by the Government of India in the mid-1950s, the drive to enroll African students in India's then 55 universities was motivated by Nehru's investment in cultivating Africans' technical capabilities as part of their training for postcolonial self-government.[8] If such a scheme sounds paternalist, it should come as no surprise. From at least the 1920s onward, Nehru's vision of a post-British India was animated by the conviction that it would be prima inter pares in the Afro-Asian world: a geopolitical concept that got its contemporary legs at Bandung, to be sure, but which was consolidating as an object of Indian nationalist commitment at least since the interwar period. The university scheme, which had brought as many as 600 African university students to India by 1965, was one of a number of technical assistance and goodwill programs directed at African youth, mainly men, in an attempt to cultivate not just their expertise, but the loyalty and appreciations of Africans for India and Indians as well. While this posture of patronage flowed naturally enough from Nehru's intellectual and political commitments to African "development," it had pointedly economic and geopolitical ramifications as well. The postcolonial Indian state was dependent on African markets—including Kenya, Zambia, Zanzibar, Ghana and Nigeria—for as much as 7% of its total imports and 8% of its total exports in 1961. This was part of a larger scheme to develop long-range policy objectives for Africa—known as "economic diplomacy"—which accelerated in the wake of the Sino-Indian war of 1962.[9] As well, by this time (that is, a mere six-seven years beyond Bandung), India's strategic involvement in African continental affairs was considered by many African leaders as a major barrier to Afro-Asian solidarity, particularly in the context of India's role in the Congo, where Nehru dispatched almost 600 troops between 1961–3 and effectively undermined any claims to India's strategic disinterest in African "sovereignty." Indeed, India's growing reputation as a neo-colonialist power where Africa was concerned strained the tenuous, hyphenated alliances between brown and black, threatening to explode the rhetorical hollowness of India's vision for cross-nationalist solidarities on multiple fronts.[10]

In *The Morning After*, unresolved tensions over the character of African development schemes, and by extension over the nature of political and social intercourse between Africans seeking "assistance" and those Indians designated as experts, are manifest as anxieties about social/sexual contact between African students and a variety of Indian women. The question of scale here is instructive: in Sen's plot, geopolitics unfolds in the daily lives and interactions of Indians and Africans in India, and in the microcosm of the Indian home and its intimate relationships. These prove to be spaces where the utopian rhetoric of Afro-Asian solidarity ("Asia and Africa are awake, aren't they? Come together, stand together, fight together, no?" are the questions that open the book) are sorely tested.[11] The story begins with the arrival of Solomon Kuchiro, a "Negro guest" of the Sharmas, an Indian Civil Service family in Delhi who have taken to sponsoring foreign visitors in their home. In a direct echo of the geographical orientation of development histories to which I alluded at the start, Shukdev remarks that they'd had houseguests "from the western world" and it was now time for "a suitable African."[12] The Sharmas' hospitality is cast as an extension of Shukdev's role as exemplar of the worldly postcolonial Indian state. As he lectures Solomon at dinner, India is the model of unity in diversity for the postcolonial world: the Gandhian example of non-violence is one that all would-be independent nations should follow. As a model for Africa in particular —where, Shukdev reminds him, Gandhi started his anti-imperial campaigns—India cannot be gainsaid. In a notable anticipation of the work of subaltern knowledge in the pedagogy of the oppressed, Solomon talks back, compelling Shukdev to recognize him not simply as an African but as a Ugandan. He informs him that he plans to use his Indian education to become a poet not a bureaucrat who will write in English (Shukdev has presumed Swahili) in order to give the language "the vigorous kick it needs". And he effectively punctures the smugness—and semi-imperialism—of Shukdev's postcolonial Indian cosmopolitanism by reminding him of India's proto-imperialist designs in the Congo and Kashmir alike.[13] Shukdev is speechless in the face of these critiques, but the real audience is his wife Sulochana, whose horror grows as she watches her husband's authority challenged and her daughter attracted by a house guest she can only bring herself to refer to as "the African" or "the Negro."[14]

From the start Sulochana provides our primary angle of vision on the encounter between Solomon and India. We watch her watch her daughter looking at Solomon, the "long-limbed natural man with hurricane hair" whom, she senses immediately, poses such a threat to Sheila that she is banished to her room the moment he crosses the threshold. Sulochana's unabashed racist anxiety, her suspicion that Solomon is a sexual predator stalking her young virginal daughter, structures the very conditions under which Solomon resides in the house.[15] He is sequestered from Sheila, who overhears the dinner conversation through the open door of her room down the hallway, and it is only a chance encounter in the garden that leads to their rendez-vous at the university via bus. Sulochana's fear of Solomon also shapes virtually all of Sheila's apprehensions of him. Intrigued by his "wild mane of hair" and his "stuttering excitable voice," she is drawn to him primarily because he enables her to rebel against her parents' bourgeois respectability and especially to critique her mother's provincialism. In so doing, Sheila reproduces her mother's racism— "Try to be nice to the Negro from the African jungle, mother . . . they don't eat elderly women"—even as she embeds it in the drama of her own individuation and development. [16] As the narrative momentum of the novel makes clear, what is at risk is not only Sheila's virginity, or her racial purity, or even her status as emblem of familial respectability. What is endangered by her flirtation with Solomon is the certainty of her mother's identity as the middle class wife: her sense of self as the companionate spouse, equal to her husband in power, decision-making and ultimately control over all the intimate spaces of the household. When faced with the intimate proximity of the African male, that household is in jeopardy; and the Nehruvian state is exposed to potential failure through contact with the very "resources" it aims to manage in the name of Afro-Asian solidarity.

Sen's portrayal of the Sharmas is clearly a send-up of a certain species of post-1947 Indian middle class identity—with its cosmopolitan desires and its transnational self-image—and in many ways it is as hackneyed as it is merciless. Not only do Sheila's fantasies about Solomon cause her to run away from home to seek refuge with her poor and plain school friend, Prabha, they cause her to reflect, predictably and superficially, on the caste and color question in her own backyard: day-dreaming about Solomon, she looks out of her window and sees the family gardeners "with skin as dark as Africans."[17] As pathetic as Sheila is, it is her mother who is the real target of the novel's satire and contempt. Throughout the first part of the narrative, her life with Shukdev is told retrospectively, as his conversations with Solomon about politics in the new India prompt memories of her early-married life. These center around her endless duties as an ICS wife, on the waning of her husband's sexual interest in her, and on her helplessness in the face of his professional ambition. Her memories also surface the history of Shukdev's rise to prominence in the Nehruvian state. Before independence, he was opposed to Congress with a hatred stoked by his anglophilia: "he was more moved," she recalls, "by the eloquence of the speakers in Westminster than by the dumb sound of famine in Bengal as thousands die"—so much so that he was awarded an OBE.[18] But Shukdev saw the arc of future and he followed it straight to a position in the new postcolonial bureaucracy. He and Sulochana abandoned their defense of the empire and wore *khadi* to a final soiree at Government House, thereby identifying themselves as the desiderata of modern independent India: the nationalist heterosexual couple. That he also began writing pieces for publication that invoked the Gita suggests how far he was willing to go to conform to what he perceived as the cultural shifts required by the new post-imperial officialdom—and how cynical the entanglement of secularism and Hinduism might be on the threshold of postcoloniality itself. Significantly, it is Sulochana and not Shukdev who emerges as the scapegoat in this pre-postcolonial history. Her memories of her husband's careerism, of his craven political opportunism, are interrupted by a phone call from one of Sheila's friends, presumably a young man, looking for her. Sulochana laments her daughter's acquaintance—"all sorts of Persians, Arabs, and Burmese and Indonesians, and, who knows, African Negroes"—all of whom her mother deems below the Sharmas in class terms.[19] When she returns to her reverie, it is to recall the brush-off her husband gave her when she tried to appeal to him on behalf of an old family friend whose father died before his pension was available. Her lament is not for her husband's callousness toward them but for the way it translates into his growing sexual indifference to her. She sees herself as "a lonely woman keeping vigil on her vanishing hold on a man . . . Shukdev, why don't you come?"[20]

When Sulochana looks at her naked body, she does not see "the droop of her breasts, her withered teats," but we do, and we presume Shukdev does too.[21] The work that the novel does to position Indian women and their sexuality in relation to the nation, and through it, to the project of Afro-Asian solidarity, is something I want to return to. In the meantime, the link between structural adjustment and male sexuality—which Kamran Ali has used to diagnose contemporary Egyptian filmic responses to family planning projects—is suggestive here, but in racially stratified terms: Shukdev is a lackluster lover surrounded by African men whose sexual intentions, if not prowess, are a pointed contrast.[22] Indeed in structural terms, the novel privileges the threat to companionate marriage as a marker of postcolonial secular identity in the person of Solomon, whose attempts to woo Sheila give dramatic force to the entire narrative. If he is horrified by the Sharmas' racism, his conviction about the nature and direction of his own postcolonial politics is ultimately fortified by the verbal tests and dinner table jousts of Delhi domesticity, a lesson in itself about subaltern insouciance when it comes to new, if recognizable, pedagogies of colonial hegemony. But Solomon is not the only one to wrestle with the convergence of political education and interracial sexual desire in the school of Afro-Asian development that India provides. Another racially charged, highly sexualized postcolonial bildungsroman unfolds through the story of Peter Kabaku, a Kenyan who has been in India for two years, having left his family to the tragic mercies of Mau Mau. The head of the African Students' Union in Delhi, he is the one responsible for placing Solomon with the Sharmas and for dealing with the fallout of Solomon's encounter with Sheila—and indeed, with all African students' problems in the capital city. If the domestic farce *chez* Sharma dramatizes the impossibility of Afro-Asian solidarity at the site of interracial mixing, Kabaku articulates a far more forceful critique of its developmentalist ambition as he narrates his own mundane experiences as an African in India.

By his own account, he was sent to India to "cultivate" Indian support for Kenyan independence, and specifically to learn the ways of Gandhian non-violence.[23] He has a picture of Gandhi in his Delhi dorm room, though he casts many a quizzical, skeptical glance in its direction. Despite having lived in several Indian cities for two years, he feels continually like a stranger. He is never referred to as a Kenyan but as an African and he knows that among themselves Indians call Africans "Negros." "Men of Bombay," he ruminates,

> [were] scurrying about . . . even those racing by him would glance at him, and in that look Peter would see a reflection of his own strangeness, of the guilt of nations and civilizations rejecting one another for centuries. Women in Bombay, stuff with nylon elegance, would look up hastily, nostrils dilating with dismay, they smelled his strange African redolence.[24]

Kabaku's experience in India is of "formal politeness and private rudeness"; a "shrinking glance, a reluctant hand."[25] As he further observes:

> Indians generally regard Africa as one country and are quite unable to distinguish between African nationalities. If you had black skin, kinky hair, and so on, you were an African, and in private conversation between Indians, a Negro from Africa. This was one of the things that Peter had learnt within the first days of his residence in Delhi. He found it easier to learn Indian prejudices than to understand India . . . not one of the Africans living in India found it any easier either. They weltered in great area of emotional chaos which made them stumble when they tried to understand emotionally or intellectually. Perhaps it was so in all Asia. Peter had begun to doubt if there was any substance to the great bolstered up theme of Afro-Asianism.[26]

All of this produces in Peter both desolation and rage that takes him to the edge of physical violence. Traveling in a train, buffeted about by unfriendly strangers, he "caught by the arm a turbaned man who had given him a push and was about to prove that he proposed to stand no nonsense even on the non-white soil of India"—when he is greeted by his official Indian greeter, Mr. Kapoor.[27]

India is not Peter's first encounter with Indians, whom he has met as prosperous but withholding shopkeepers in Nairobi.[28] But if he arrived in Delhi with any doubts about the possibilities of cooperation, we are not privy to them: from the start he is broken by India itself, a country "so keen to teach" but which only "breeded doubts," doubts that pierced, "arrow-sharp," "somewhere deep into his being."[29] Peter's story is one of disappointed expectations: the promise of Afro-Asian solidarity that propelled him from Kenya to India has been exploded, encounter by cumulative encounter, on the streets of Bombay and Delhi. Peter does not have a poet's eye. Where Solomon sees the "pink and gold" of Delhi's evenings from the lush garden of the Sharmas' house, he sees only "the filtered gloom that seeped through the skylight" and smells only the combination of "stale detergents and spices that pervaded Constitution House," where he sits nightly in his dingy room.[30] And it is in the context of failed connections with Indian women that his desperation is most fully articulated. Kapoor introduces him to Kumari Bhatia, part of his India welcoming party, and she gives him what he recalls as a canned speech about the "new bonds of intimate friendship" that Afro-Asian connections like theirs will nurture; yet he sees that she cannot look at him. She takes him to his residence hall to sign forms and he represents her as casting him an almost defiantly sexual look: "wetting her lips, [she] stood apart, silently, frequently hiding the brief swollenness of her breasts under the folds of her silken sari... after a while they all said namastay in the interest of Indo-African friendship."[31] Once he's left alone, Peter falls into a tortured reverie, lamenting the impossibility of such a coupling with Kumari. Indians knew nothing of Africa beyond "dim pictures" of savagery. "He would not rationalize the effects of these attitudes on him as a Negro. He was tormented, the sadness in him became larger and larger, like the lengthening darkness of the evening outside."[32]

Solomon offers Peter, and the reader, the possibility of less fatalistic interpretations of India's impact on visiting Africans—without, significantly, redeeming the promise of Afro-Asian solidarity per se. He comes to Peter's dorm room to complain about his stay at the Sharmas, offering this devastating analysis of his role in the postcolonial project.

> I must run, Guru Peter, the Brown Sahib and the Pink Lady must be getting ready for dinner, and I must present myself as the sacrificial goat for a second lecture on the greatness of Gandhi et all (sic) . . . India must pour out the all burden of her myriad years . . . Bye Peter, and don't worry, Africa is black enough, I couldn't make it blacker, not to my Indian hosts, anyway . . .[33]

Solomon has not just a deeper political analysis than either the Sharmas or Peter, he understands and is willing to name its complex racial dynamics, as his reference to the differentials of color in his hosts' household attests. That he sees through Sulochana is particularly telling; it suggests that he knows how the grid of race and gender and youth is about to play out, even if he doesn't anticipate Sheila's escape to her friends and ultimately, her rejection of him as a chapter in her own bildungsroman. His is the most provocative politics of all. As he tells Sheila, "you know . . . it's not a question of Indian or Ugandan culture; it's really a question of the interplay of cultures . . . neither your father, nor Mr. Pande [an Indian dinner guest] . . . is really very Indian. Each one of them is an interplay of several cultures. . . Frankly speaking, I don't quite get them. They seem to be unreal."[34] In the end, although the aspiring poet is wiser and lighter hearted than the "official builder of Afro-Asian dreams," as Solomon calls Peter, Peter takes no comfort in it, fearing for Solomon's fate: he dubs him "too much alive in India" for his own good.[35]

Although the sexual drama between Sheila and Solomon is the event that ostensibly prompts the novel's "morning after" English title, in fact the novel derives its impetus more precisely from the story of Peter's failed encounter with both the Nehruvian educational project and the transnational solidarities promised by Afro-Asianism—failures refracted in intimate detail through interracial sexual attraction and repulsion. Peter's time in Delhi is marked by sexual scandal, and he is ultimately driven from the city by his own indiscretion: an affair with an Indian woman for whom he feels a combination of lust and contempt—and whom he gets pregnant, much to his horror, not least because he has a wife and child at home in Kenya. Significantly, his shame centers not around conjugal betrayal but around the suspicion that the woman—who is unnamed in the text—has been planted by the Indian government to seduce him and ultimately to discredit Kenyan nationalism in the eyes of both Indian officials and the larger postcolonial world as well. Kabaku's bitterness and anger about the failure of the promises of transnational racial solidarity, here and elsewhere in the novel, routinely run through his experiences of failed interracial sexual relationships and more generally through the racism he cannot escape in any quarter of urban life. He ends up exiling himself from Delhi in an Indian village where a government agent, a Miss Asha Dutt, is organizing the local school as part of rural development work. There too there is sexual attraction, this time unfulfilled, but it is to her that he confesses his loathing for India, his disappointment in the Gandhian way and above all his sense of embodied alienation from Indians by virtue of being viewed by them as a primitive black man—an experience that not only shames him, but renders him politically powerless. He asks for her help in getting a passport back to Kenya because, in his words, "I would rather be arrested and hanged in Kenya than vegetate in India." And when she refuses to aid him with the passport he says bitterly, "be assured I do not want your help."[36] In the end Dutt does come to his assistance, seeking a sexual relationship that he promptly rebuffs. At the end of the novel both Sharma and Dutt—each agents of the Nehruvian state project of African uplift and transnational solidarity—have been resolutely rejected in circumstances shaped if not determined by the failure of intimacies of all kinds.

Although they are not the novel's narrative drivers, Indian women act as critical indicators of the failure of India's development schemes and of internal fractures in the nationalist project nonetheless. Prabha, the school friend with whom Sheila finds refuge when she seeks escape from her mother's watchful eye, is too poor to go to university. She lives at home in "squalor" and is caretaker to several siblings as well as maid of all work around the house. Her mother does not speak English (though we are told she takes pride in her daughter's ability to do so), placing her well beyond the frame of the Sharmas' blinkered ICS vision. Beetles "moved lethargically in the corner" of the room Sheila is ushered into and for all her myopia in other respects, she can see that food is scarce.[37] Prabha is thin as a reed, and Sheila notes that she herself "looked like a wrestler" in contrast—a comment that underscores her narcissism in this recessive and marginal space of the postcolonial nation her father is so determined to see as atop the post-war world.

Prabha is, moreover, the reasoned and insistent voice of traditionalism and arranged marriage in the book. As she tells Sheila,

> 'Marriage is the most important thing for a girl. Just imagine how many girls have dared to marry out of their caste even. And to be sure, many of these 'love' marriages turn out to be unhappy. Marriage is more than a personal event . . . it is a social event, and it needs social sanction to stay happy. I mean, I can't think of marrying against my parents' consent. I act, I depend on them entirely.'
>
> 'I know you do. You are old-fashioned. I don't.'

'It's alright if you can find a man in your own caste. But if you go too much outside, you take a great risk. How do you know the man will love you and care for you after the first few years?'

'But how do you know the husband your father will find for you will love and care for you forever?'

'He will be under a social obligation to take care of me. I will love him because I must. And he will love me because I am his wife.'

'As simple as that?'

'Isn't it? I don't know. It's so difficult. I prefer not to think about it.'[38]

Prabha's interrogation of Sheila then begins to revolve around the kind of provider Solomon would be. "Where will you live? Will Solomon get a good job? ... what will happen to your children? Will they be Hindu or Christian? Indian or African?" she wants to know, impatiently but forcefully. "You must not act out of impulse," Prabha warns her. "It is true times are changing. But not much. I mean, not *so* much."[39]

In contrast to the Sharmas' dinner table, where race is spoken about openly and discussions of racial difference between Indian and Africans are a badge of postcolonial Indian worldliness, Prabha relies on the language of caste as a screen for race, which is a word that cannot, apparently, be spoken between them even in girlish conversations about Sheila's African paramour. (That "so," in her last "I mean not *so* much," signifies the unspoken but voluble link between caste and race). Sheila, for her part, is suddenly alive to the comparison; she sees Prabha's life as her own if she marries Solomon, the sordid conditions of an "outcast/e" life transposed only too readily in her mind onto the dim and frightening future of interracial marriage. It's a future whose backwardness she cannot even contemplate. "Slowly and invisibly like the hand of clock, a huge panic opened around her. She could never, never ... she felt sick at the thought. She pushed it away with an effort."⁴⁰ Sheila returns home and gives up on the idea of Solomon not because she is persuaded by Prabha's arguments about arranged marriage or even because she wants to preserve the social fabric of the new nation. She is repulsed—literally and aesthetically—by the fate of permanent, unenviable and utterly unimaginable underdevelopment to which she believes a marriage between herself and an African man would consign her.

Just because Sheila does not walk away from Solomon for the sake of the nation does not mean that her scene with Prabha is without its Nehruvian target—in this case, the upward mobility mentality of an ICS class that requires subalterns (national and transnational) *and* the channeling of female heterosexual desire as well.⁴¹ I read Sheila here as part of the novel's critique of the Sharmas and the cultural assumptions entailed by their class status: as evidence of the imaginative limits which the first generation of postcolonial Indians is bequeathing to the new nation. Thus a dominant interpretive thread of the novel is the power of endogamous Brahaminical conjugality to forestall the threat of Afro-Asian intimacy, if not in the name of developmentalist biopower (Sheila's choice seems more aesthetic than political), then certainly in its service. In her capacity as vulnerable daughter Sheila also enables the novel's savage take on the way pollution complexes shade into and are fed by racial anxieties at the site of sexuality—a take that brings the brand of normative conjugality at the heart of elite postcolonial Hindu/secularist visions into full view.

A similar critique of how instrumentally women as always already conjugal subjects-in-the-making are put to use in nationalist projects operates through the figure of Miss Dutt. She is the woman Peter encounters doing village development work. That assignment—which involves getting community buy-in for the construction of local schools—is not a plum job but, as it turns, out, a highly gendered form of consignment. For Miss Dutt is a former anti-colonial terrorist who shot at a British governor and was jailed for life as a result.⁴²

As Shukdev Sharma tells Peter when he first approaches him about finding him a scholarship,

> There was a huge commotion about it all. Even the Mahatma who condemned her act could not accept the brutal sentence awarded ... her. And Panditji who was then a young barrister ... without much practice though—was a member of the committee to organize the legal defence. Quite a drama. We released her soon after freedom.[43]

It's worth lingering on the gender politics of such an account. In many respects it's a canny rendition of the "coercive protection" to which Indian women were subject in colonial and nationalist discourses in late colonial India.[44] And of course it captures Gandhi's infamous ambivalence about women activists in the nationalist movement. Above all, it anticipates what we come to understand as Shukdev's deep misogyny, here aligned almost insouciantly with the attitudes of the founders of independent India. Would an Indian civil servant utter such thoughts in any other conversation than with an African man living in India in order to study Indian history? This is collaborative patriarchy of a kind rarely seen in either colonial or postcolonial contexts, one that takes place not only over the body of an Indian woman but through a critique of the questionable gender performances of India's patriarchs themselves ("quite the drama" suggests hysteria or, at the very least, failure to manage an appropriately masculine response).[45] It is also, significantly, the most casual, untroubled exchange of interracial intimacy in the whole novel, which suggests that when it does happen, Afro-Asian solidarity is a homosocial experience at the expense of a brown woman—all in the name of the transfer of postcolonial knowledge in a developmentalist register.[46] That this is the moment when Peter recommends Solomon to Sharma as a houseguest (and he agrees) suggests the complexity of sexual trafficking at the heart of this developmentalist narrative and the urgency of attending to the structural conditions of possibility for Afro-Asian solidarity *tout court*.

Despite these homosocial currents, and of course because of them as well, at issue for Sharma is the desire of Miss Dutt to be an agent of the developmentalist regime versus his determination to use her as part of his personal and professional experiment in technology transfer. Rather than a scholarship, Shukdev offers Peter useful work in the village to which Dutt has been assigned. The dialogue that follows is worth reproducing in full:

> 'What's she doing in the village?'
>
> 'Oh, a lot of things. Messing around, I suppose. She wants to work in the villages, and she has a lot of pull with some ministers and there she is, like a political supervisor. Our development officers don't like her. She is constantly pregnant with ideas, and each is a great discovery to her. It makes things rather difficult at times.'
>
> 'I see.'
>
> 'But she is not entirely useless. She has a lot of sincerity, and she loves the villagers and they have some regard for her. And she is utterly honest and upright a little too much, I should say, of a moralist. And I should better warn you, rather ugly looking.'
>
> Shukdev Sharma laughed again. Peter remarked,
>
> 'Not a very tempting image.'[47]

Shukdev's contempt for Dutt operates on several levels. He scorns her work as quaint and irrelevant to the postcolonial nationalist work he does and to his self-styled ICS cosmopolitanism. And he deems her ugly in the bargain. But it is precisely the limitations of her physical attractiveness combined with her active mind ("pregnant with ideas") that fits her for the drudgery of village work *and* makes her the perfect match for Peter. Her purported lack of beauty, in other words, has a negative value that Sharma converts into the work of development on two fronts—creating the opportunity for a species of interracial cooperation, if not intimacy as well.⁴⁸ "I am going to arrange for you to work there," Sharma tells Peter, because he knows Peter will find Dutt a "very interesting woman." "Peter's nerves suddenly froze. 'I am not interested in any woman, Mr. Sharma,'" he tells his would-be benefactor, "Not that kind of woman, Kabaku," Sharma laughed. "You will like to know her . . . you are a revolutionary. She is one too, or has been. You may like one another."⁴⁹ In keeping with the novel's impulse to target the developmental hubris of the Nerhuvian middle class, we see Sharma here articulating a misogynist contempt for the former anti-colonial woman revolutionary, a concept mimicked by the state's conviction that her place is 50 miles from Delhi, where she can be left to "mess about" harmlessly and presumably to no great social or economic effect either. Sharma's assumption is that her capacity as a woman, limited from the start by her ugliness, has already been wasted so that village development is the perfect rubbish heap for her. Her passions having been "diverted"—by prison but also, it is implied, by the exigencies of asexual Hindu girlhood—her body is "brackish and stagnant as a backwater". "Unused," it had become "over-blown."⁵⁰ Even so, Sharma virtually pimps her out to Peter, relegating them both to the internal frontier of Indian domestic underdevelopment where they can talk their idle talk and perhaps even connect in other ways —though he laughingly assures Peter that's not at all what he had in mind. For Sharma, Peter belongs in the recesses of national domestic space with a failed revolutionary from India's pre-postcolonial past. Should Peter learn lessons from that revolutionary history that prove useful in the Kenyan present, so much the better. It simply ratifies Sharma's conviction that Africa's future will be made by drawing on history that India has already passed through, developed out of, and can now export as a kind of technopolitical good to desperate black colonial subjects whose destiny is apparently to approximate the political, economic and socials forms of their Indian betters.

In fact, what happens as a result of the partnership between Miss Dutt and Peter is that a dam is built in "her" village. What he seeks is proximity to some Gandhian "spark"; she, by her own admission, has none, but what she does have is a river that needs a dam. The local development officers are not interested; they have no common cause with the villagers, and as Subir Sinha's work has shown, it is their disinterest that is partly responsible for the stagnation of many rural community development initiatives by the mid-1960s.[51] Here, however, it is Peter who listens; together, they strategize. By way of enlisting his help, Dutt remarks:

> You are an African. In Kenya and other African countries you must be thinking of mobilizing human resources for nation-building activity. We are poor in everything. But we have people. This is our wealth. And we must utilize this wealth. If you come with me and tell these government people that a dam is what this village needs most, they will probably act.[52]

He agrees; "and, as the two sparks of idealism joined, a file was born."[53] The file (that post/colonial emblem of bureaucratic inertia) takes a while to become a dam, but with Dutt's perseverance, the villagers' labor—and Sharma's intervention—the dam is built.

Despite the psychic cost for all concerned, technological improvement does occur as a result of this experiment in Afro-Asian solidarity. It happens not in Africa but in India itself, through the mobilization of a very specific form of biopower—rural labor enabled by an Indian woman who, according to the text, "is the zealous and over-excited mother" of the project.[54] That a dam is the outcome of "the morning after" reveals how self-interested the state's schemes for south-south cooperation actually are, not to mention what the real object of redistributive justice in a transnational mode actually is (Indian rather than African development per se). Meanwhile, the fact that Miss Dutt is crushed by Kabaku's return to Africa—she literally drops to the ground, wordless and immobile—is something we get only a brief glimpse of. Compared with the Sharma women, she has very little interiority indeed. She is all politics, all business: even knowing Peter is from Kenya, and that she has a fatherless child, all she wants to talk about is her dam. What we do know is that the villagers who saw her simply talking to Peter felt "she was digging the grave of her virtue."[55] It's that virtue—independent of her "beauty" and also, of course, sacrificed to her personal happiness—which ends up redeeming Sharma's experiment in Afro-Asian cooperation, making his career (he's now Secretary for the Ministry of Irrigation and Power) and putting an Indian village on the map of postcolonial modernity. He has, as his wife cynically observes at the start of the novel, continued to move "with the times."[56]

All of which leads us to ask, if *The Morning After* is evidence of the vexed intimacies of Afro-Asian history—an archive, as I have been suggesting, of its intersection with and constitution through postcolonial schemes of national/ist development—what kind of critique does the novel end up producing, if any? As we've seen, it comes close to reducing the Sharmas and the Nehruvian state to caricature; that, together with its indictment of the self-serving character of state-sponsored Afro-Asian schemes, produces its own political effects. Are these undercut by the fate of Miss Dutt? She is not a figure of patent ridicule like Sheila; yet the pathos of her sacrifice goes unremarked in any metanarrative sense. What of Sen's representations of Solomon and Peter? They surely act as foils for each other—one a noble dreamer, the other a bitter and tortured man of action nearly destroyed by his postcolonial encounters with India and Indians—and in that sense, they are interdependent rather than fully sovereign subjects. As interdependent are the Sharmas and their African "students," with whom they are locked in a classic Saidian embrace: Shukdev needs Peter to ratify his sense of techno-cultural and racial superiority; Solomon, for his part, is the perennial "thing of blackness" that repairs an always faltering heteronormative bourgeois identity, whether Sulchona's developed or Sheila's developing one.[57]

On the other hand, Peter is perhaps the most developed character in the novel. We are given his life-story before Delhi in vivid detail and have the chance to see how his hard-won political education was formed in part through his relationships with whites —as servant and love interest of an English master and a bar singer respectively. This renders him a kind of equivalent to Shukdev: he too began with western colonial models and has turned, now, in lateral direction, to models across the decolonizing world. If Peter is to be considered the main character of the novel, and I think there is a case to be made for this, that certainly diminishes the significance of even a semi-farcical figure like Shukdev as the stable center of the novel, or the nation. Indeed for some critics, simply acknowledging Peter as the protagonist may answer questions about the success of the narrative in getting outside the verticalities of racialized power it so assiduously maps. It is he, after all, who represents, through his own witnessing, the *realpolitik* of a post-Gandhian independent India to readers. This might be read as yet another way in which he services the postcolonial nation, though as distinct from Nehruvian state: he stands in that gap, rather than in the hyphen of Afro-Asian solidarity per se.

And yet it's hard not to be struck by how elemental a character Peter consistently is. He ranges, hungry and detached, across the urban and rural landscapes of India. He has a sexual appetite that is often described without irony or critical distance; the scene of sex with an Indian prostitute reproduces stereotypes about the size and power of his "manhood" with nary a trace of self-consciousness about the stereotypes entailed by such images.[58] Whereas Nehru's descriptions of African representatives at Bandung as "heftly and giantly persons" may be said to have gentrified African masculinity, Peter is not rendered in such terms.[59] He has no more or less a redemptive view of women than Shukdev, whose opinion of Dutt's ugliness he unapologetically shares. His wife Wachira makes a brief appearance, and that occurs only in Peter's memory. As the mother of his child, the recipient of many letters home detailing his work in India and, ultimately as the victim of brutal local violence that ends her life, she is an iconic cipher of African womanhood—which tells us as much about Sen's capacity for complexity on the subject as it does about Peter's character, if not more. Peter thinks confusing though lustful thoughts that arise from chaotic city experiences where he is thrown up against Indian women in ways he's unaccustomed to; but his sinister, predatory and aggressive masculine power is not gainsaid in the text either. Even though we have a genealogy of why this is so, and we have his agonized account of being perceived in this way in India, Peter is, for all intents and purposes, the personification of the threatening African male that Sulochana Sharma projects onto Solomon. And more. As he broods over the African students whose sexual dalliances with Indian women he's had to deal with—including charges of rape against them—he was thinking "of Afro-Asian solidarity, and of a woman. Pretty. Soft. Nipples as big as figs. Not Wachira, oh God, no!"[60]

The African students accused of rape (allegedly of an ayah) deny the charges and share Peter's view that they have been set up "because we are black people . . . because we are Negros."[61] As one says to Peter in an echo of Peter's own words to Asha Dutt, "I would rather get killed in Africa than live in India." The novel itself is agnostic on the veracity of the rape charges or the students' interpretation of them, as it is on the potency of Peter's sexuality. Though the links between his sexual urges and his turn to violence are run through his traumatic Indian experiences, Peter's temperament—his "African personality," to use a phrase from this period—is not individual, it is predictive as well. Where Solomon smells flowers and sees rose-tinted skies, Peter smells dirt and is compelled not just by what's happening in his homeland, but by the belief that violence is the most appropriate response to the last days of European colonialism. Although he wears his Gandhi cap almost to the end of the story, it is very much "askew"; and once back in Kenya, he "joins a wandering band with stolen guns. They chew the tapioca roots, and their beautiful white teeth shine like beacons for their fellow men."[62] This is close to jungle imagery, and the narrative puts no distance between us and the tropes of blackness, primitiveness and savagery it conjures. Kabaku "is the modern Memnon of ancient Ethiopia," likened to Ulysses it is true, and carrying "the ever burning torch of freedom" as well. He is also indistinguishable, "a tiny figure, struggling on, black as pitch black as golden light, blacker and brighter than anything else in existence." It would be easy enough to conclude that this brutal and brutalizing end is the result of Peter's failure to follow the Gandhian way.

And yet the novel makes indisputably clear that such a project was doomed from the start because of how anachronistic—as in, temporally out of joint—that pathway is in a free India already operating under a different set of assumptions of what postcolonial modernity should look like. To offer such an interpretation is not to suggest that Sen's novel is an apologia for an India that was; for *The Morning After* is not a paean to either village India or its urbanity. I think that the most scrupulous way to read this ending is to argue that, in the novel's own terms, the tragedy of Peter Kabaku is that he was caught in the crosshairs of an Afro-Asian solidarity movement that could not exceed the structures of pre-postcolonial *or* postcolonial development in which it was invariably ensnared. By plotting Afro-Asian solidarity as a series of failed and/or doomed romances, Sen compels us to see those failures as the result of long histories of uneven development, some of them set into motion by earlier forms of imperial power and others shaped by the regimes of racial difference and sexual purity developed in and through the nationalist postcolonial imagination and its administrative apparatus.

This returns us, appropriately, to the original Bengali title of the novel, *Rajpath, Janpath*—two boulevards in official Delhi with gendered names and foundational significance, not least because they were the avenues through which colonial power flowed and postcolonial power was transferred. On the opening pages they are described as

> two roads on which brown and browner people move. Raj, the rulers, and Jan, the reproducing mass who is ruled. One is the path of great power, where all sights are set; the other, the source and victim of that power. For centuries the two hardly ever met except as strangers. Now they meet, collide and collude still very largely as strangers.[63]

What are we to make of this metaphor, which may or may not be read as channeling the narrative voice of Peter Kabaku? Given the events of the novel, are we to understand India's relationship to Africa as a gendered version of this layout, with Africa the female partner, the Queen of Queensway—both source and victim of postcolonial India? Or, given the fact that Solomon flirts with Sheila by calling her the "Queen of Sharma" (a play on "Queen of Sheba," and on the blackness of her royalty as well), do we conclude that desire doesn't happen across "hyphens" because it throws them into chaos and disarray?[64] Or that there is no intimacy to be had, just purely political/bureaucratic exchange, as happened with the production of the dam: technological assistance between strangers? Or that there should not be a pretense to intimacy in this form of exchange because it is doomed as a result of pollution complexes and miscegenist fears?

I favor the latter interpretive route, but not because I think the novel is fully in control of its own citationary apparatus. To be sure, the hollowness and cynicism of the postcolonial developmentalist regime is caught out; and Peter gets to be a hero in both India and Kenya. But—unsurprisingly, and in keeping with so much postcolonial work—the gender politics are in a temporal lag, a perpetual out-of-jointness, with the postcolonial political critique that the novel plots. Who's on top in *The Morning After*? Indian and African men, who oversee a development scheme carried out by an Indian woman and nameless villagers and, in the case of Peter, take up arms and produce "real" political results that can be partly attributed to the success of boot-camp training in the new postcolonial metropoles of the Third World. If he felt grateful for it, as some future Zambians who attended the 1956 African Students conference in Delhi said they did, it is not addressed in the novel.[65] And if we range *The Morning After* alongside other novels by Africans from the 1960s and 1970s that feature African students in western universities, we find little of such gratitude either.[66] But Afro-Asian solidarity is not just a(nother) means of consolidating male domination across racial communities. It effectively mimics the protocols of earlier forms of British imperial power, this time by managing respectable brown women so that they service a transnational ideal and yet remain vulnerable but ultimately sexually unavailable to black men.

The exception here is the Indian prostitute with whom Peter has sex. African women are all but invisible, and (some) Indian women are, yet again, the mothers of the nation, but hardly in a self-fulfilling or self-directed way. The latter—Sheila and her mother as well as Miss Dutt—represent a kind of stunted excess of the developmentalist postcolonial state: they bear the burden of failed development in ways that Indian men collaborate in and African men like Peter witness as a template for gender relations in the newly postcolonial world that, together and apart, they are all building. There is, in fact, agency aplenty here, at least for the men. For Peter is not just invited to India by the Nehruvian state, he is *sent* by Kenyan nationalists who want him to profit from the model of Indian freedom. He is in fact a "camouflaged student" sent by "leaders of the revolution" ostensibly "to look for the Gandhian way in Indian life," but equally to garner Indian support for the Kenyan cause.[67] Though his Kikuyu comrades are a shadowy presence in *The Morning After*, the novel is clear that there is desire on both sides for this experiment in what Peter, at his gloomiest, calls "Indo-African" friendship rather than Afro-Asian solidarity per se.[68]

It's worth noting here that Sen himself subtitles the English version of his book "a non-novel," explaining in the "Introduction" that it is "not even remotely a translation" of the Bengali original, which was "an immediate success, and has run into ten printings, most probably because it was the first attempt, in Bengali, since India's independence, to write a serious political novel." He goes on to note that many readers suggested an English translation, and that one, an Indian agricultural engineer working in Nairobi, actually sent him a complete English version. So, *The Morning After* moved, quite literally, in the very circuits of Afro-Asian exchange it chronicles, and that we have it in English is partly due to the materiality of its embeddedness in post-Bandung history. In that sense, the novel itself is at once a vehicle for and an indictment of the abortive hopes for this particular experiment in cultural diplomacy designed to personify Afro-Asian solidarity. While one might imagine that such hopes were born and dashed over the course of several decades, the novel plots this as a much more self-contained arc of historical time, so that the unraveling of Afro-Asian solidarities on the ground are made known to Bengali audiences as early as 1960 and later (1973) to its secondary audience, English readers. According to Dhruba Gupta, so widespread was the fear of marauding African male sexuality in Indian cities as a result of popular Bengali work like Sen's that an Ethiopian student was actually refused housing by a landlady as a result.[69] Did events in Uganda—which, according to one contemporary, signaled the "shock of unrequited love" for Indians vis a vis Africans—prompt the translation?[70] While these connections remain speculative, what is clear is that *The Morning After* is not just an archive: it is an intimate counter-history of Afro-Asian solidarity.

That very project—along with the romance of racialism the novel critiques without ever fully exceeding—compels us to acknowledge that in order to model transnational methods at their best, we need research and narrative strategies that challenge presumptions of racial confraternity that may have been shaped at Bandung but are not borne out by what unfolded in "Afro-Asian" experience in its wake, at least not in self-evident ways. We need histories that refuse all of Bandung's pieties and romances and break, finally, from its presumptively fraternal narratives, if not its epistemological grasp. Above all, we need methods and frames that can capture the wide variety of what Paul Kramer, in his study of African and other state-sponsored "foreign" students in the US in the twentieth century, calls the "dangerous non-alignments" of the postcolonial Cold War landscape.[71] Kramer's work, together with that of Maxim Matusevich on Africans' role in "the official ideology of Soviet internationalism" during the same period, points to a broad comparative framework for thinking about modern fictions of (uneven) development, especially given the tense interactions that state projects committed to the diffusion of African youth (mainly men) in a variety of post/colonial contact zones apparently sponsored.[72] The point here is not simply to linger in the tensions of cross-racial encounters, though historicizing their negative affective traces is, as I have suggested, indispensable to a fuller account of their political significance than has been acknowledged. The real challenge is to figure out how Afro-Asian history might be positioned—sited and cited—as a touchstone for a critical appreciation of transnational methods and what those maneuvers might mean for narrating accounts not just of the 20th century's postcolonial politics, but of the racial and sexualized global orders that shaped it as well. The point is, in short, to begin to frame feminist, interpretations of Afro-Asianism, where feminist signifies a skepticism of its romances and a critical insistence on the energy which the occlusion of *sexual* politics continues to lend to *postcolonial* politics in the contemporary present.

Notes

1 Chanakya Sen is the pseudonym for Bhabani Sen Gupta, a prolific and often controversial political commentator (1921–2011).

2 Raghavan Iyer, ed., *The Moral and Political Writings of Mahatma Gandhi*, v. 2: *Truth and Non-Violence* (Oxford: Clarendon Press, 1986), p. 296.

3 http://timesofindia.indiatimes.com/articleshow/1641567.cms

4 See Subir Sinha, "Lineages of the Developmentalist State: Transnationality and Village India, 1900–1965" *Comparative Studies in Society and History* 50,1 (2008): 57–90; and Manu Goswami, *Producing India: From Colonial Economy to National Space* (Chicago: University of Chicago Press, 2004).

5 Chanakya Sen, *The Morning After: A Non-novel* (Calcutta: Academic Publishers, 1973). All citations henceforth in the text. Shukdev is sometimes spelled/printed as Sukhdev in the English text of the novel but for the sake of consistency I use Shukdev throughout my essay.

6 Jed Esty, "The Colonial Bildungsroman: *The Story of an African Farm* and the Ghost of Goethe," *Victorian Studies* 49, 3 (2007): 407–30.

7 Quoted in [no author] *Nehru and Africa* (New Delhi: Indian Council for Africa, 1954), p. 15.

8 Richard L. Park, "Indian-African Relations," *Asian Survey* 5, 7 (1965): 350–58. For an account of African Studies in Delhi, see Wayne Fredericks [Ford Foundation], "The Department of African Studies, University of Delhi," *African Studies Bulletin* 3, 2 (May 1960): 16–18. The Department was established in 1955 and its curriculum included a two-year M.A.

9 Ajay Dubey, *Indo-African Relations in the Post-Nehru Era, 1965–1985* (Delhi: Kalinga Publications, 1990), pp. 36 and ff.

10 The stakes of this relationship were high in the age of Bandung where Chou En Lai challenged India's ambition to be the leader of the "new world of Asia." Then as now, China loomed large in the geopolitical landscape of Afro-Asian connection and "solidarity," most often as a wedge rather than a hyphen because of the ideological tensions between capitalism and communism that beset postcolonial Indian relationships with Africa—not least in terms of the competition for talent, markets, human resources and of course, the very terms through which "Afro-Asia" was to be dominant in Cold War postcolonial world. For a detailed analysis of China's strategic interest in

Africa see Philip Snow, "China and Africa: Consensus and Camouflage," in Thomas W. Robinson and David Shambaugh, eds., *Chinese Foreign Policy: Theory and Practice* (Oxford: Clarendon Press, 1994), pp. 283–321.

11 Sen, *The Morning After*, p. 1.

12 *Ibid.*, p. 119.

13 *Ibid.*, pp. 27–28.

14 *Ibid.*, pp. 5–24.

15 *Ibid.*, p. 3.

16 *Ibid.*, pp. 26, 21, 7.

17 *Ibid.*, p. 25.

18 *Ibid.*, p. 47.

19 *Ibid.*, p. 50.

20 *Ibid.*, p. 56.

21 *Ibid.*, p. 49.

22 Kamran Ali, "Myths, Lies and Impotence: Structural Adjustment and the Male Voice in Egypt," *Comparative Studies of South Asia, Africa and the Middle East* 23, 1–2 (2003): 321–334.

23 *Ibid.*, p. 14.

24 *Ibid.*, p. 10.

25 *Ibid.*

26 *Ibid.*, pp. 10–11.

27 *Ibid.*, p. 10.

28 *Ibid.*, p. 81.

29 *Ibid.*, p. 9.

30 *Ibid.*, p. 8.

31 *Ibid.*, p. 13.

32 *Ibid.*

33 *Ibid.*, p. 17.

34 *Ibid.*, p. 74.

35 *Ibid.*, pp. 16, 15.

36 *Ibid.*, p. 155.

37 *Ibid.*, p. 138.

38 *Ibid.*, p. 134.

39 *Ibid.*, p. 135.

40 *Ibid.*

41 I am grateful to Jed Esty for this suggestive observation.

42 Sen, *Morning After*, p. 118.

43 *Ibid.*

44 See Ashwini Tambe, *Codes of Misconduct: Regulating Prostitution in Late Colonial Bombay* (Minneapolis: University of Minnesota Press, 2009). pp. 63 and ff.

45 See Lata Mani, *Contentious Traditions: The Debate on Sati in Colonial India* (Berkeley: University of California Press, 1998) and Gayatri Spivak, "Can the Subaltern Speak?" in Cary Nelson and Lawrence Grossberg, eds., *Marxism and the Interpretation of Culture* (Urbana: University of Illinois Press, 1988), pp. 271–315.

46 See Eve Kosofsky Sedgwick, *Between Men: English Literature and Male Homosocial Desire* (New York: Columbia University Press, 1985).

47 Sen, *Morning After*, p. 119.

48 For a discussion of women's beauty as added value see Dipesh Chakrabarty, *Habitations of Modernity: Essays in the Wake of Subaltern Studies* (Chicago: University of Chicago Press, 2002), p. 121.

49 Sen, *Morning After*, p. 118.

50 *Ibid.*, p. 62.

51 Sinha, "Lineages of the Developmentalist State."

52 Sen, *Morning After*, p. 40.

53 Ibid.

54 Ibid.

55 Ibid., p. 36.

56 Ibid., p. 48.

57 I borrow here from Kim Hall, *Things of Darkness: Economies of Race and Gender in Early Modern England* (Ithaca: Cornell University Press, 1996).

58 Sen, *Morning After*, p. 110.

59 See above, "Introduction"; originally cited in Judith M. Brown, *Nehru: A Political Life* (New Haven: Yale University Press, 2003), p. 261.

60 *Morning After*, p. 107.

61 Ibid., p. 104.

62 Ibid., pp. 167 and 171.

63 Ibid., p. 3.

64 Ibid., p. 70.

65 "Nehruji . . . urged us, when we went back home, to dedicate ourselves to the liberation of Mother Africa, a continent which Nehruji said had suffered the most from outside exploitation . . . Nehruji had a marked influence on whatever small part we played in liberating our country." Mr. S.T. Kapwepwe, Mr. N. Mundia and Mr. Sipalo, "Ministers in Dr. Kaunda's Government," quoted in *Nehru and Africa*, p. 23.

66 I am thinking here of Tayeb Salih, *Season of Migration to the North* (London: Heinemann, 1969), among others. His novel is especially germane as it stages a very dramatic encounter between an African student and a white woman that shapes the whole plot. Thanks to Jed Esty for encouraging me to think about this question.

67 Ibid., pp. 14, 101.

68 Ibid., p. 13.

69 Dhruba Gupta, "Indian Perceptions of Africa," *South Asia Research* 11,2 (1991): 172.

70 Prem Bhatia, *Indian Ordeal in Africa* (Delhi: Vikas Publishing House, 1973), p. vi.

71 Paul E. Kramer, "Is the World Our Campus? International Students and US Global Power in the Long Twentieth Century," *Diplomatic History* 33, 5 (2009): 776.

72 Maxim Matusevich, "An Exotic Subversive: Africa, Africans and the Soviet Everyday," *Race and Class* 49, 4 (2008): 57–81.

CHAPTER 4

HANDS AND FEET

Phyllis Naidoo's Impressions of Anti-apartheid History (2002–2006)

I am Indian by Tradition,
By race I am African.
I am an African Indian in Africa.
   Tshque Haracharan, 2004[1]

I begin with something of a fanciful image. Picture Phyllis Naidoo (b. 1928) standing somewhere on Grey Street declaiming: "Do not call me an Indian. I am a South African." Maybe she is standing outside the Victoria Market or in front of the Juma Musjid Trust Madrassa. She could be somewhere on Commercial Road, or Pine, or as far from Grey Street proper as Sastri College, where she was a student. She might be deep in memory, recalling, like the character of Nithin Vania in Aziz Hassim's novel *The Lotus People*, the cinemas that used to be on the main thoroughfares of Indian Durban—the Vic, the Royal, the Avalon—and the businesses now shuttered or long gone—"Dhanjees Fruiterers, Victoria Furniture Mart, Kapitans, that noisy Royal Tinsmith Company."[2] And yet if you know Phyllis Naidoo even a little bit, you will hardly be surprised to learn that when she makes her claim to a South African identity at the historic heart of Afro-Asian community on the southern edge of the Indian

Ocean, she thinks as far afield as Pietermaritzburg and Cape Town and Harare, well beyond the territorial limits of Grey Street, Durban, Natal or even South Africa itself. She reaches, in short, for what Annie Paul calls "the outer-national."[3] Though forged in these precincts, her geopolitical imagination—like her career as an anti-apartheid lawyer, activist, teacher, fugitive, ban-breaker, saboteur, good Samaritan, cynic and unrelenting comrade—is as expansively local as it is affectively global. Phyllis has managed the simultaneity of "I am not an Indian" and "Grey Street is the crucible of South African history" by planting her feet firmly on its pavements and extending her hand to all those comrades who traveled through the anti-apartheid movement via its "far ocean jetties"—which, incidentally, is the aptly named imprint of one of her Durban publishers as well.

This is partly because Naidoo's politics have been aspirationally non-racial: a term common to South African history but one that most people outside it—myself included—tend to trip over, because it doesn't translate readily into the identitarian terms through which race is often apprehended. Naidoo thinks history and does history not beyond race or in spite of race but squarely in the face of it: in a mode of solidarity that may have begun as a means of doing political resistance but has ended up as the basis of an anti-apartheid historical method. It is as historian that I want to think about Phyllis Naidoo here, by focusing on her Grey Street quartet (primarily volume 1, *Footprints in Grey Street*) and, in passing, her monument to the 1956 treason trialists, *156 Hands that Built South Africa*.[4] Taken together, these writings add up to a radical form of biographical and autobiographical memory and a remarkable archive of Afrindian solidarities and frictions in the context of struggle history.[5] The fact that even this work, produced by an anti-apartheid activist, exhibits some traces of the citationary practice that is the subject of this book testifies to the challenges of historicizing relationships between Indians and Africans—and, more generally, of desegregating the literal and imaginative spaces in which highly charged racial histories have unfolded.

Naidoo's narrative mode is ostensibly biographical. *Footprints* contains dozens of sketches of people from all walks of South African life: journalists, anti-apartheid leaders in brown, black and white, prisoners, teachers, workers and a host of everyday, "ordinary" people too. Each chapter focuses on one figure, typically providing a kind of life-cyle account of him or her that intersects with movement politics in more or less detail, depending on the person at hand and on the type or amount of information available. Take, for example, the chapter on Abdul Khalik Mohamed Docrat, born 1915 in Kathor, Gujerat. Naidoo narrates his life story, including his arrival in South Africa in 1930, his opening of a shop in Victoria Street in 1939, his participation in the Liberal Study Group that met in a warehouse in Ajmer's Arcade. She details the political work he did that got him imprisoned during the war and his role in the internecine politics of the NIC; his detainment during the State of Emergency, his multiple bannings, his harassment by the Special Branch, and the clandestine political work he continued to do in those trying circumstances. Though this is not true for every person logged in the book, Phyllis has clearly interviewed "Doc," and she quotes liberally from her question and answer session(s) with him.[6]

> Docrat explains that after 1940 Indians were the predominant organized working class. As new wartime industries were set up, cheaper and unorganised African labour was preferred. So the job shifted from Indians to African[s]. Legally, Indians having struggled now enjoyed trade union rights, while Africans were denied these rights. Much conflict resulted with the declining Indian workforce and the rising African workforce. It was engineered not by the parties involved, but by the racist establishment.
>
> They were workers, not Indian or African. Divide and rule was a British preserve, it spread to trade and industry and other aspects of Natal life.[7] (51)

Throughout, Naidoo's admiration of Doc is evident: though he only had standard four schooling, he was never intimidated by "highly educated" people and he remained an avid reader. In fact, he took to selling books during the 1940s, walking the streets and collecting all manner of newspapers in the process. "This unsung, irascible archivist," she tells us, ". . . collected posters, delegate tags, leaflets, petitions, press clippings, stickers and other struggle paraphernalia … of the political events in our country. He was our walking political dictionary." Pointing us to his archive and archiving these details simultaneously, Naidoo herself never strays far from her Grey Street theme: "he had a great network!" she exclaims. "Great footprints." [8]

As must be clear even from this short digest, Naidoo's interest in Doc is not merely biographical. She uses his life story to create a narrative of struggle politics that is at once unerringly class-conscious —"our solution is socialism and the Freedom Charter is the first step towards this"—and unswervingly interracial—South Africans "are workers, not Indian or African." In this case, she attributes to Doc a non-racialist attitude that involved patronage for, outreach to and worker solidarity with Africans. If we hear in this account an echo of Naidoo's own self-professed relationship to the South African Indian question, it is in part because his testimonial voice blends almost imperceptibly with her narrative voice across the course of this passage. By citing Doc, she sites his political work as a commitment to class over race: a project that presumed no difference between brown and black. In what follows, we gain further insight into what non-racialism might mean in concrete terms, in lived experience, for politically-minded Indians of Doc's generation:

> Doc with Peter Abrahams, Fred Carnerson and Sarah Rubens attended an ANC meeting in Pietermaritzburg around 1940/1. Rev. Mthimkhulu was in the chapel . . . There were objections to Indians and Whites attending the meeting. But this modest bunch claimed, 'We are here to support you, not to oppose you.'

'Our activities were centered around the ANC objectives and not ... ANC activities,' says Doc. We helped each other. The Liberal Study Group penetrated all levels of organisation in Natal, the Natal Indian Congress, Trade Unions, Ratepayers Association,Communist Party and Commercial concerns.[9]

Although cooperation across organizations did begin to occur after 1947 (the famous Doctors' Pact), ANC membership was initially closed to everyone but Africans—a fact that complicated political alliances across race and community and signals the kinds of frictions that shaped the political lives of Doc and his peers. Nelson Mandela addresses these frictions in his autobiography, remembering both how the impressive passive resistance campaign of 1946–47 was "confined to the Indian community" and how disagreements about the nature of non-racial cooperation shaped the ANC leadership and strategy.[10] Ismail Meer, for his part, remembered Mandela as "part of the fraternity of exclusivist Africans who kept us at arm's length politically" in the 1940s—though Meer refused, interestingly, to call this racism.[11] Determined to register these complexities, Naidoo cites examples of how non-racialism played out among a variety of people of South Asian descent repeatedly in *Footprints in Grey Street*, to such a degree that it's not too much to say that the project of archiving the complexity of "race relations"—brown-black but also brown-white and to a lesser degree, brown-coloured—gives narrative logic and momentum to the text as a whole. To borrow from both Sharad Chari and Njabulo Ndebele, Naidoo's work is a powerful example of the "incitement to ... forms of realist, personal narrative" and its politics of racial knowledge in the wake of the unfinished business of apartheid's dismantling.[12]

The cast of characters Naidoo evokes is so diverse, and her evidence for each subject so different, it's hard to say that any one citation is emblematic, let alone that there is a singular citationary method at work. Yet patterns do emerge, chief among them the story of what we might call upward political mobility in radical terms: the bending of the arc of radicalism toward freedom fighting through personal sacrifice, struggle and suffering. Take, for example, her focus on Poomoney Moodley, whom Naidoo follows from her time as a young woman through her work at FOSA (Friends of the Sick Association, which is where Phyllis met her) through the hardships of her entire work life to her refusal to turn state's evidence to her imprisonment to her relentless work for prisoners on Robben Island. In many ways an inveterate historian of family, Naidoo gives us Poo's genealogy—including her "rise" from a large family of indentured labor origin (complete with names and vital statistics of all Poo's siblings) whom she supported "in this hell of grinding poverty" by washing "dirty whites' clothing"—so that we can fully appreciate the historical significance of Poo's political work. Naidoo is especially focused in her narrative on the Hospital Workers Union, of which Poo was part of the executive. In the process we learn of Poo's role in the SACTU (South African Trades Union) strike as well as of the global impact of that strike and its success vis a vis improved conditions and wages for the majority of workers. We also witness Poo's determination, her tirelessness, in the face of detentions and her own ill-health, which included a "dead" or disabled left hand. In March 1960 Poo lived with Phyllis: "we slept in the same room in my one-bed roomed flat. After reading she fell off to sleep. Her breathing caught my attention. She struggled to breathe, like an asthmatic clawing for breath. A weird painful whistle accompanied each breath and her contorted body told at what cost she lived. Sleep did not come easily."[13] But Poo was undaunted, selling banned newspapers, leafleting, "collecting cakes, baking, you name it"—Phyllis attests—"she gave equally to these tasks," with an indefatigability that literally stunned Phyllis into silence, as when she came upon Poo leafleting in Hoosen Buildings in Queen Street: her dead hand held the leaflet, while the right hand posted them into the boxes."[14]

Poo's story offers a finely textured, even intimate, view of how anti-apartheid politics happened on the ground.

> The 90 day detention hit us in 1963. Poo was detained. Rushing over to check, [her sister] Peggy confirmed that Poo had been arrested at King George and brought home to her Carlisle Street flat that Peggy and Poo shared. They searched the whole flat. Search is probably the wrong word. There was nothing orderly about the search. The wardrobes were ransacked, everything was thrown all over the flat while they taunted her about clothes belonging to comrades. She had picked up their laundry and they were expected to pick it up.
>
> Attorney Rowley Arenstein made representation to get Poo her medication. Peggy was allowed to take her a foam rubber mattress, sheets and pillow. From her detention cell she sent a message to Peggy saying:'DON'T WORRY. DON'T PANIC. DON'T TALK TO ANYBODY[']. Wow [comments Phyllis], this girl!
>
> In the pocket of her gown we found a letter from Billy Nair. It was yards and yards of toilet paper. The SBs missed it in the search.
>
> … My home was subject to similar searches, so I did not keep this priceless piece of history. Peggy [,] scared to incriminate her sister[,] destroyed it. Am I sorry? DAMN!
>
> Daily Poo was taken from Mayville to Wentworth. Women in detention fear both torture and rape. During one session Poo started screaming. Dawood Seedat in detention was exercising in the yard outside and heard Poo scream. While jogging past the window where he thought she was, he shouted—DON'T LET THE BASTARDS GET YOU DOWN POO. Dawood was clobbered and lost his privileges of exercise time. Poo was strengthened by Dawood's voice. It's wonderful knowing you are not alone.
>
> She was released not being charged or called as a witness … so many UNSUNG HEROINES AND HEROS in the struggle for justice in our country.[15]

In this we have a glimpse of what may have never been "properly" archived, at least not beyond this account. And other things are left unspoken as well, including the possibility, at least, that Poo was sexually assaulted in prison.

As is the case in nearly all Naidoo's entries for South African Indians, Naidoo cites Poo's interracial credentials as the heart and soul of who she was, and as the basis of her comradeship in and with Grey Street. We learn that like Phyllis, Poo was MK (Umkhonto we Sizwe = "Spear of the Nation," the armed wing of the ANC) and that she used her own meager funds to get cash, cards, letters and whatever else she could to MK comrades in prison, to whom she was known as "Cousin Poo."[16] "The money was not from any organization, Dependant's conference or its likes. It was money from her pocket, a small and overstretched pocket! Curnick Ndlovu, Jason Kuzwayo, Sunny Singh, Natoo Babenia, Dip, etc., etc. I know, because I had to despatch this money."[17] Poo's determination extended to comrades once they got out of prison; her sense of connection was deep and did not, Naidoo implies, admit of racial divide or difference. Naidoo recounts the story of how she and Shadrack Maphumulo (member of the General Workers Union, later killed in Swaziland) needed to use Poo's car to meet up secretly with Stephen Dlamini (factory worker, leading trade unionist and Natal ANC member), to whom Poo had smuggled many things—a radio, shoes, weekly papers—while he was incarcerated. Poo insisted on going, was rebuffed but insisted; and in the end she and Steve had a "precious reunion."[18] What was the nature of their friendship? Naidoo does not say. She does, however, tell this story not once but twice in the book, signifying its significance for Grey Street and the political contributions of its inhabitants to the South African cause.

Naidoo's insistence on salvaging Poo's memory is rooted in her own frustration that unlike other, more famous revolutionaries—such as Ruth First, whose death by car bomb (1982) was memorialized 10 years after it happened—Poo was forgotten. "WHY" Naidoo asks, in capital letters. Though she never says so in these terms, the implication is because she was a minor character, a poor woman, a nobody in the public record of the struggle. Naidoo witnesses her death by cataloguing her "short, distinguished and courageous life . . . Nearly 35 years of her 56 years was given to the liberation struggle"—thus effectively ensconcing Poo in anti-apartheid memory as both an ANC stalwart and a fighter "for justice for all in our country."[19] For Naidoo, Poo serves as an example of an anti-apartheid worker who was neither Indian nor African. She cites her, in other words, as an ordinary South African in the context of a lifetime of anti-apartheid struggle and as a symbol of a non-racial form of struggle commitment personified.

Yet even this tribute is not the full extent of Naidoo's counter-history, her bottom up account of Grey Street struggles. She closes the chapter on Poo with a long quote by Che Guevara that applies directly to her friend:

> The fight for freedom, human dignity traverses a long trail. Many fall, others borne by strong feeling of country and fellow men, stride a lonely road, making painful decisions unfalteringly. Love for this hallowed cause indivisible, spiritualised possessing the fullest measure of humanity, of justice and truth. An incorruptible spirit, absolute integrity, aloofness from all compromise, a daily struggle, transforming love of humanity into concrete deeds and acts that serve as a mobilising force and an example.[20]

Poo's entry ends, finally, with the salutation "Hamba Kahle Kanna." "Hamba Kahle" is isiZulu as well as isiXhosa for—variously —"stay well," "good journey," "good bye." "Kanna," we learn earlier in this chapter, is a Tamil term of endearment, one that Poo has used with Phyllis while speaking to her on the phone while Phyllis is in exile. The juxtaposition of Che's words with this linguistically hybrid farewell epitomizes the Indian Ocean world cosmopolitanism that I have suggested is characteristic of Naidoo's historical sensibility: at once local, but complexly so, and global, though not simply in geographical terms. What links Poo's life with Che's exhortation and ultimately with Phyllis' linguistically mixed farewell is less the spatial parameters of political affiliation than the capacious—and heterogeneous, even promiscuous—geopolitical imaginary of world historical resistance and revolution. It's on these foundations that the critical genius of Naidoo's "impressions" of South African history is built in *Footprints in Grey Street*, and upon which her interpretive intervention in struggle history restlessly sits. It also marks Naidoo as a particular kind of patron, someone with the linguistic knowledge and political authority to cite Poo's role and to position her as a player in a "people's history" of anti-apartheid in relation to the local, the national and the international arena—a emancipatory narrative that, in her view, presumes non-racialism as a universal value coming out of global worker struggle.

Poo Moodley is just one of many comrades whose biography ends with the Hamba Kahle chorus. Her biography is just one of many ostensibly "small stories" that make up the first volume in Naidoo's quartet, a volume which is literally teeming with detailed genealogies of footsoldiers who lived their lives full throttle in the struggle but remain below the sightline of even South Asian resistance histories. Take Rajaluxmi Pillay, known as Ray or Rajes or Bones, whose father, T.V.R. Pillay, was president of the Kimberley Branch of the Tamil Vedic Society and secretary to the Cape Coloured People's Association. Raj became assistant secretary to the Students Representative Council, Black Section, University of Natal in 1966, joined the ANC a decade later, and went into exile in 1986 in Zambia. Or Subbiah Moodley, who was confronted by two SB officers at Springfield Teacher training College about his student protest activities in 1964.

> He was ordered to pack his bag and was bundled into one of 4 cars that awaited him. Any plans to escape were met with its futility. He was taken to his home, a flat in Willis Road.

'You don't want a description of my shocked mother who opened the door and was rushed by a bevy of policemen.' They searched the house....

'I was not left behind to help her clean up the flat or more importantly, to comfort her. I shall take that pained and shocked face to my grave.'[21]

Nor are Naidoo's chosen subjects by any means only people of South Asian descent or even those who hail from Grey Street itself. Phyllis' history is expansive, and she's unfazed by the territorial limits of Indian Durban proper. What she asks of the inclusion of Denis Godlberg, she asks of any number of comrades featured in the book: "What does this have to do with my Grey Street when he belongs to Cape Town?"[22] If a comrade was in "our neck of the woods," literally or in spirit, he "belongs firmly in our Grey Street area and his footprints are firmly embedded in our democracy." In many respects, hers is an arguably non-racial account in terms of numbers and also in terms of method, capacious to a fault and generous about the boundaries of Grey Street, which stretch to accommodate a variety of political hues as well.

And yet the question of historicizing interracial connection and politics is not so easily resolved. Indeed, among the most compelling—and vexed—questions of anti-apartheid history is the nature and extent of political collaboration and social intercourse between Africans and Indians, whom both the colonial state and the Nationalist government aimed to pit against one another—and whose histories have mainly been written in parallel rather than in tandem. *Footprints in Grey Street* is bursting with biographies of Africans which, in turn, reveal their work in the struggle and their relationships, both casual and organized, with Indians as well. What Naidoo does is to supplement extant apartheid narratives with what Lisa Lowe has called, in another context, "new narratives of affirmation and presence."[23] I want to underscore here that that supplement is not of

"Africans" but of an Indian South Africa history by stories of African-Indian encounter and solidarity. That Africans traveled through, worked in and otherwise populated Grey Street and its adjacent spaces in "Indian Durban" is a historical fact.[24] That African freedom fighters working side by side with Indians are affirmed in *Footprints* as a critical part of Grey Street history might be considered an act of desegregation. Take Bongi Dlomo, born to Kesiah and Jeremiah Makhoba in 1936. Bongi was their third child, and Naidoo rehearses what she knows of all 6 brothers and sisters, as well as of their father who believed passionately in education. All 6 become professionals, thanks in part to the good offices of the eldest brother, Ellie, who learned bookkeeping and took responsibility for those who came behind him. Several also gave their lives for the cause. Breaking the third wall as she often does in *Footprints*, Naidoo calls for a collective witness to this collective accomplishment: "can you believe that this rural family has produced these giants in education, nursing, and the political struggles that ushered in our democracy"[?] One brother, Pius, was detained under the Terrorism Act; another, William, was also detained, tried and acquitted. Having left the country for Maputo he was assassinated in 1981 with 14 others. "This and more," Naidoo announces with pride, "is Bongi's family." Bongi, for her part, trained to be a nurse and worked at McCord's Hospital. She fought against separate nursing registers in 1957; her husband Albert Dlomo was an ANC member and sentenced to 3 and a half years on Robben Island in the way of the 90-day lass in 1963. Eventually he was released and the family moved to London, where they lived for 20 years, still working with and for the ANC.[25] Naidoo's message is clear: Bongi belongs in Grey Street, if not to it as well.

In fact, Bongi is one of a number of African women who appear in *Footprints* whom Phyllis knew well, worked with, respected, and admired—with a quality of feeling that sometimes borders on reverence. In a historiography that is largely endogamous when it comes to narratives of racial struggle, and in which evidence of cross-racial alliances between women is comparatively scarce, *Footprints* cites any number of examples of cooperation and collaboration between women of Indian and African descent. It's a plain-speaking record of the daily work of cheek-by-jowl struggle shared by women of many races in the context of late 20th century South Africa.[26] Phyllis' account of Dorothy Nyembe is notable in this regard. A "stalwart in the struggle," Dorothy was active in the anti-pass law campaign, in SACTU and in the women's demonstration in Cato Manor in 1959—an event well known because of "that famous award winning photograph of the women being bashed by baton wielding policemen."[27] Although she admits to being unsure if Dorothy was present at the equally famous 1956 women's march, Naidoo confirms that "she was there" in Cato Manor 3 years later.[28] Not only was she there, she was a major force in the resistance to the removals and in the beer hall conflagration of 1959. Nyembe reportedly urinated into a vat of beer to drive home women's challenge to male authority and pleasure, an act that "quickly became legend." While Iain Edwards quotes Nyembe several times in his 1996 essay on the beer hall riot, her name is not in the book's index—which makes Naidoo's insistent citation all the more urgent.[29] As Naidoo relates, the beer hall was only part of Nyembe's legacy: she was a member soon after MK was founded, for which she was arrested and served a 3 year sentence. In 1969 she was again charged (this time with 9 others) and sentenced to 15 years, which she served fully in Kroonstad prison.

Here as elsewhere we learn how Phyllis' own political life intersected with that of her subject:

> I was a practicing attorney by the time she started serving her sentence at Kroonstad. With the help of a fellow prisoner she wrote me a note complaining she was starving. She could not eat the large mealies served for lunch, as she had no teeth. She needed dentures, iPlease

> send me R200.00,i the letter read. I dutifully obliged. We could not starve Dorothy to death.
>
> Her daughter, married to a policeman, found it extremely difficult to visit her political mother. I found a Methodist minister who had come to a conference in Durban and asked him if he would visit Dorothy regularly. He agreed. Please let me know if she has any needs, I instructed him. He could not, for when he visited her they (the Security Branch) would watch him... .
>
> On her release from prison in 1985, Natal was ablaze. She could not live in her home at Kwa Mashu, but lived at the Durban railway station. She was cold and lying on the floor at the railway station did not help much. When she visited Harare she lived with me. She took my warm slippers saying she needed them more than I did.
>
> Dorothy was awarded the USSR Peoples' Friendship Act, a prestigious award. She was one of our M.P.s in the National Assembly in our new democracy in 1994.
>
> Death robbed Dorothy of her courageous life on the 17th December 1998. She will leave no further footprints for us to emulate, but she has left us a precious memory of indomitable courage.
>
>> Hamba Kahle Dorothy[30]

Beyond inscribing these lives in and as antiapartheid history, vignettes like these serve a number of purposes. In the first instance, Naidoo registers Afrindian solidarity at the ground level of the struggle in ways that official political histories of the period have rarely done, in part because they are more concerned with establishing party/political timeline or even more simply, with identifying links and intersections and collaborations from what is admittedly an extraordinarily fragmented archive, one reliant on newspaper accounts and ephemera of the kind that was not necessarily preserved in the heat of battle, as Poo's toilet-paper note to Billy Nair, above, indicates. Prison memoirs have been produced at a great rate in the last decade, even as the main protagonists grow old and pass away; these are largely accounts of fraternal relationships among famous and/or infamous, undeniably powerful ones though clearly not the sum of anti-apartheid history. *Footprints in Grey Street* adds depth and structure of feeling to these, registering a host of more invisible histories, between men and women and between women as well.[31] As significant is the record of patronage Naidoo leaves, the pride of citation in her account of Dorothy—a pride that extends to Naidoo's suggestion that Indians and Africans struggled together against the regime and that women shared sacrifice and suffering equally. To be sure, if Dorothy herself had views on the commonalities of this struggle we are not vouchsafed them. In this sense, the citationary apparatus Naidoo uses is not just top-down, it can work to gloss as well, in this case by occluding if not erasing from view any alternative accounts of political "solidarity" by Africans themselves.[32]

In part because she knows the stakes of claiming a shared political consciousness, Naidoo's draws repeatedly on her own anti-apartheid work—the dailyness of the struggle in her own life and the politics of intimacy, interracial and otherwise—in order to give legitimacy to her account of common struggle. Take the story of Cynthia Phakathi, which Naidoo tells at length in a chapter dedicated to Cynthia, is exemplary in this regard. Here is Phyllis:

> One afternoon in 1974/5, I found a young mother and her baby in my office. She was looking for a job, and she was there with her baby at her breast, waiting to be interviewed.
>
> I asked, 'Are you looking for work?' 'Why bring your baby with you? What employer would give you a job with a baby?'
>
> 'I have no one to look after my son. I don't want to wean him unless I have a job. Then I can pay someone to take care of baby and be able to buy milk for him.['] She was dehydrated and asked for water. The humidity did naught for her comfort. She had the most disarming smile.
>
> 'Have you worked before?'

CP said, 'I worked for A.J. Gumede in his Pinetown office and I have been fired.'

'Oh heck!'

Does she know that A.J. Gumede (Archie) is my partner? If she has been fired in one office, what makes her think she will be employed in his Durban office?

'This is serious,' I tell myself. 'What do I do?'

... I rang Archie and enquired why he had fired Cynthia? She was in my office applying for a stenographer/cum secretary job.

The general gist of his reply was, 'Oh Phyl, don't touch her. Her work is atrocious. She never gives you neat typing. Very shoddy work! I am a patient fellow. Your standards are very high. You will quarrel with her and that wont be good. This Indian/African thing will come up and you will be hurt. Say no now, and put paid to this matter.'

'Thanks Archie.'

I tell Cynthia exactly what Archie had said about her ... 'I cannot employ you with my partner complaining about your work,' I said.

'But you are a mother and you know our problems[,]' she responds.

She had touched a nerve there. Did I know Cynthia's problems? Many was there a time that I had to find a home to leave my children. Sometimes my baby Sanna was brought to school and left on the staff room carpet with napkins and bottle, while Bugani our child minder attended her quack, or funerals. No crèche facilities existed in our time. On our miserable income, we employed child minders at a pittance. Both our wages were a disgrace.

We agreed, Cynthia and I [,] that we would have a trial period of two weeks. If she was not happy she could leave anytime. I would give her two weeks. The pay I cannot recall now. It was not Oppenheimer's fare. I paid my workers more than he did his mineworkers... .

In her first week, I presented Archie, our convenyancer, with documents for his signature. 'My goodness, this is lovely work. Do you have a new typist?'

'Yes,' I replied [,[] calling Cynthia to come meet Archie.

Both looked at each other in shocked silence.[33]

As an account of inter-racial politics, this anecdote is rich indeed. Phyllis' patronage of Cynthia on the grounds of shared motherhood upends the "professional" relationship between legal partners, though if it produced ill will between Naidoo and Gumede we are not privy to it here. Cynthia's story also tells us about Phyllis as an employer of Africans, in several settings (office, home), her sense of solidarity over wages and her colloquial dismissal of her childminder's medical practices as well. The rest of the chapter on Cynthia details how her office work came to overlap with, or blur into, childcare for Phyllis' children "daily after school," as well as how her office work involved not just typing but also serving coffee and tea and biscuits to all the clients—including a host of luminary Robben Island-returned "friends"—as well. Naidoo tells us that Cynthia and Phyllis' messenger, Rita Zuma, "were studying part time in the evenings. It was part of the contract of work." This blurring of paid work and "political" work, broadly conceived, had fateful consequences. On the day that the decision for Naidoo to leave the country was taken, it was Cynthia who told an unidentified caller to the office, "I am not sure whether Mrs. Naidoo has gone to Pietermaritzburg, many people, even the police are waiting for her." With typically dramatic flair, Naidoo tells us: "She was talking to me." [34]

Cynthia's story as told here has a recursivity in *Footprints* that's worth dwelling on. For by the time we get to it thirty pages or so into the book we have already encountered it in a much more condensed form in the very first chapter, which is dedicated to Archibald Gumede. That chapter opens with a paean to Gumede's political chops, his bravery, his brilliant legal mind, his fearlessness and his sacrifices for the cause. "How do I know all this?" she asks us. "easy! I was his partner. His proud partner." Naidoo goes on to detail their partnership in offices on the 7th floor of CNR House, Cross Street—the heart of Indian Durban.

It was the only practice in the whole country that offended the racist government. They wanted to separate us. Archie was an African and I was of indentured Indian stock. But our common humanity outweighed any imposition by racists from wherever they came. I remember a call from Robert Sobukwe in Kimberley where he wanted help in a matter in the Durban Courts. He chose us for he found it strange that an Indian and African would be in a partnership in law. When I told him I suffered under restrictions similar to his, he dropped the phone on my ear.

Our partnership gave articles of clerkship to several clerks[;] some completed[,] others went on to complete elsewhere: Geoff Abrahams, Jeff Radebe, Sangaree Govender, Mduduzi Guma, Sivi Reddy and others come to mind for the period 1973 to 1977.

I was banned and house arrested, restricted to Durban magisterial area. Nobody would offer me a job and setting up a law practice as ... expensive... It was a struggle to be admitted as an attorney. I discussed this with Archie.

My lack of court practice was also a stumbling block due to the banning orders. (The Law Society used this to keep me from practice, but Judge Harcort held that not all attorneys practiced in court—company lawyers, etc.)

Archie suggested he would do the court work, while I worked at the office. I had to get permission to leave Durban to go to Pinetown. The magistrate refused me permission to work in Pinetown.

Archie immediately offered to give me R300.00 per month to start my office in Durban. That is how we started Phyllis Naidoo and Archie Gumede. My politics did not attract the rich in society, but mainly the poor. We made a comfortable living.

His conveyancing papers were typed in the Durban office. Archie checked and lodged papers. As soon as we were able to stand on our feet, Archie stopped paying us. But we went on acting as his agent in Durban. It was a precious relationship and it was poor Archie who reached out to me when nobody else would touch this politico. Archie was deeply religious and I was an atheist. Thank you Archie.[35]

It's at this moment that Phyllis turns to the story of Cynthia. Some detail is added: "When I told him it was Cynthia [doing the typing], he would not believe me. He called her in and asked her why she did not work as well for him. She reminded him she was still working for him." In this version, Cynthia and Phyllis seem to have much more of the last laugh on Archie, showing how gender solidarity could interrupt cross-racial alliances and empower an African woman not just to prove her worth or get her job back but to tell her African male employer that she "still" works for him. Naidoo does refer to Cynthia's loyalty to her in this version, but the tribute is to Cynthia—and to Naidoo's joint work with Archie as well. "She studied and read for a B.A. degree," Phyllis recalls. "We, Archie and I[,] were very proud of her."[36]

Clearly the 7th floor Cross Street offices were as much a social as a political hub; they epitomize how intricately linked those two domains could be, especially where personal, embodied interaction between Africans and Indians was concerned. All kinds of "politicos" sought legal aid, vital services and basic nourishment there. As Naidoo remarks, "one cheeky attorney visiting said, 'Why don't you remove your nameplate and simply say 'Phyllis' coffee shop.'"[37] People congregated there after their prison release, bumped into each other in pursuit of business or a warm drink, and might even find temporary employment, as George Naicker did in the Pinetown branch after 14 years on Robben Island.[38] Examples of how news passed through this informal clearinghouse, of how hands were extended and lives connected, abound in *Footprints*. It is not too much to say that as a desegregated and desegregating space, this law practice—conceived initially out of a commitment to lending a hand to a comrade in need and located in the heart of both the commercial area and the imaginative precincts of Grey Street proper—was central to the political education of both major and minor players in the anti-apartheid movement.

The same was true in Nelson Mandela's first law office in Johannesburg, where his secretary was Zubeida Patel, wife of Cassim Patel of the South African Indian Congress. "She was without any sense of the colour bar whatsoever," he wrote in his autobiography. "She had a wide circle of friends, knew many people in the legal world... [and] brought a great deal of business through the door."[39] Like Mandela's workplace, the offices of Gumede and Naidoo are an important and overlooked space of shared political work, reminding us of how haphazard and transient such formations could be. Dissolved by Naidoo's forced exile in 1977, the partnership spawned numerous personal associations that exceeded its short life and the boundaries of the nation as well, as the stream of visitors to Phyllis in exile from those days eloquently testifies. Yet in Naidoo's multi-layered narrative of the Cross Street offices, we also get a glimpse of how cross-hatched—by gender and class—such political experiments could be as well. Cynthia emerges here as a product of the joint political project that Phyllis and Archie created in their Cross Street experiment: she's cited as an object of their common patronage, and evidence of their interracial partnership as well. Cynthia stands for Afrindian solidarity, but not wholly on her own terms. She also stands in for a fuller discussion of Gumede himself and for the unique nonracial partnership Naidoo had with him. Like some other Africans cited in *Footprints*, Cynthia tells us something about Naidoo's "possessive investment" in blackness, her determination to shape a narrative of common politics via the political development of African workers—and perhaps about the limits of reading interracial intimacies, even political ones, from a public history like *Footprints* as well.[40]

The workaday character of the Cross Street project at the height of anti-apartheid activity stands in powerful contrast to other, more performatively staged displays of Afro-Indian solidarity after 1994. This contrast is evident in Naidoo's chapter on Gladys Manzi, who was honored (as was Phyllis) in 1998 in Cape Town as one of the sixteen Freedom Fighters of South Africa, part of independent India's 50th anniversary commemorations. Manzi was literally wrapped in a shawl given to her by the Indian High Commissioner at the ceremony. Though she recounts the occasion with considerable pride, Phyllis moves quickly back to the guts of the struggle—to Gladys' sacrifice for it and to the ways they cooperated in the heat of small battles, especially on behalf of the families of Robben Island prisoners.[41] Here as elsewhere, Naidoo's focus is on the education of the contemporary reader, to whom she wants to bequeath a sense of the sacrifice and struggle of ordinary workers in the cause, their recognition by the Indian state notwithstanding. I interpret this not as a rejection of the Indian government's patronage—its "citation" of Indian and African women as South African—but as an attempt at studied indifference to it, and a return of the reader's attention to the broken bodies, like Gladys', upon which the struggle was built.[42]

In an echo of the emphasis on Srenika's re-education in Ansuyah Singh's 1960 novel, *Behold the Earth Mourns* (explored in chapter 1), the political education of the reader is, in fact, a recurrent concern for Naidoo in *Footprints in Grey Street*. She resolutely, and more than once, calls the book a "collection of short stories of my comrades" that she hopes will be "improved with your continued research"—challenging at once the strict facticity of her account and pointing to its provocative power: for her history is anecdotal, open-ended and above all dialectically engaged with the reader. That reader, whom she directly addresses and invites into the book as an engaged interlocutor, is called upon from the very start to participate actively in these "short stories" not merely as a spectator, but as a potential historian, a fellow researcher even. Naidoo imagines her *Footprints in Grey Street* as something akin to a sprawling Wikipedia entry—to be read but also to be shapeshifted by readers in the process. With a canniness of historical timing that is characteristic of her entire oeuvre, she did so at the very same historical moment that that now famous virtual enterprise was taking off at accelerated global rate, advertising itself as the newest, most flexible and most democratic form of knowledge available.[43]

As for capturing the reader's attention, Naidoo does so in several different ways. She uses strategies of direct address; she refers to various archives to which students of the movement can turn for more information; and of course she makes use of her own research to flesh out the stories of those subjects she has singled out for consideration. Ever conscious of her role as provider of basic struggle knowledge, she frequently cites books as references, like Eddie Roux's *Time Longer than Rope*, and citing chapter and page from others, like *Organize or Starve*, a history of the SACTU.[44] Nor was she above inserting a timeline or two to tell the story of a political life, as she does in her chapter on Judson Diza Kuzwayo.[45] If we take her exhortations about the spatiality of struggle seriously—the simultaneity of its local rootedness with its multiple, expansive imaginative geographies—we must also admit that for Naidoo, refiguring Grey Street as the diverse, mutli-racial, kinetic and generative locus of anti-apartheid activity is, for her, utterly indispensable to the political *re*-education of the reader she conjures. Though it's impossible to say for sure who that reader might end up being, I think her intended audience may well be people of South Asian descent who she believes are unaware of the long and deep history of interracial politics, social intercourse and resistance: those who think Grey Street—as an urban space and as a metaphor—belongs only to Indians. Her emphasis on ordinary people of modest means who became struggle workers suggests too that her intended reader may be Indians of a middling class who might be inclined to disidentify with workers, black or brown.

If this is the case, the spatial ramifications of reader re-education in *Footprints* can be understood in several ways. As I have suggested, Naidoo is determined that students of anti-apartheid appreciate the contributions that Grey Street made to the struggle, and she envisions its ambit not technically, in a literal cartographic sense, but geopolitically, in the sense of encompassing a global anti-racist, class-based solidarity struggle. The turn from India as a locus of Indians' diasporic political identity toward South Africa as the site of their political commitment is crucial to this vision. It involves not just a re-direction of the gaze from one nation-state to another but the repudiation of a sense of difference from Africans in South Africa itself, *and* a concomitant embrace of a shared project of democratic struggle that is at once non-racial and anti-racial, where anti-racism means a rejection of logics of difference based on skin color, yes, but also on segregated histories of the struggle itself. The real take-away of *Footprints* is not simply that all the people named in it threw their lives into work for the cause, but that they did so across color lines in ways that have not been visible even in the wake of apartheid's end. Making the geographies of interracial solidarity an indisputable component of the narrative arcs and logics of struggle history is not just Naidoo's contribution to accounts of anti-apartheid's pasts, it is a clarion call for South African history itself to de-segregate by recognizing the limits and possibilities of reconciling conventional truths about race with how politics unfolded on the ground in the decades leading up to 1994. This call is at the heart of Naidoo's racial politics of citation. It's also what makes her citationary practices the equivalent of "uplift," with the mixture of goodwill, patronage and hierarchy that that entails. For Naidoo, then, bringing Afrindian stories out of obscurity and into history means desgregrating Grey Street and repositioning it on the grid of "South African" history writ large. It means citing a history of interracial cooperation that presumes an equality between communities and even individuals via a process that, nonetheless, carries with it some imprint of the frictions between brown and black that were characteristic of the struggle itself. And, as we have seen, it means surfacing mainly select Durban experiences as part of a "national" narrative of anti-apartheid history.

Naidoo's own political education is the grounds for this revisionism, and we learn every bit as much about how it was forged in the crucible of Grey Street and environs as we do about all the people who passed through during the long years of struggle, resistance and revolution. Most of this is an incidental feature of the micro-portraits, as we have already seen in some of the anecdotes she relays. Rarely does she address her own family of birth, save through her entry on her brother, Devadas Paul David, and even there she treats him more like a comrade than a sibling.[46] Yet Naidoo's autobiographical voice and the histories it entails are inextricably linked to the slices of biographical evidence she materializes—for big and small actors alike.[47] Her chapter on Luthuli, one of the first in the book, begins with an account of her own student days at the Non-European Section of Natal University in Durban, when Naidoo and some of her friends decided they wanted to form a branch of the ANC, c. 1957–58.

> We were whites, Africans, Indians and one Coloured. Ernest Gallo, Khalakhi Sello and myself were mandated to raise the matter with the ANC. We set up an appointment to meet Chief Albert Luthuli at his flat in Carlisle Street. Together we walked down Grey Street to the ANC office in Lakhani Chambers in Saville Street. When we got to the area near to the taxi rank near what was then a restaurant—Kapitans, some taxi drivers (28) sitting on the pavement said in Hindi, 'Look at our nation girl walking with these Africans.' They did not use that word of course. I told Chief what was being said. He stopped and said most politely that we were three students, and he was Chief Luthuli of the ANC. They stood up shyly and held their heads down. Chief asked if they were South Africans. They shook their heads. 'So we are, all four of us,' said the chief. They raised their hands to thank Chief. We chuckled as we walked on. The meeting was held at the ANC offices. I remember Joe Matthews and M.B. Yengwa were there to listen to us. After giving us a good hearing, they said they would raise the matter and return to us. They did, saying that the ANC constitution had provided only for African membership. So while the Freedom Charter was accepted by the Congress Alliance, it had not been adopted by the ANC. When it was done, it led to the break away and formation of the PAC on the 6th April 1959.

As a result we formed a Human Rights Committee at Natal University. Jonathon Paton and George Sewpersadh were among some of our members.

Later we were going to a meeting in Port Shepstone, when Chief pointed out two homes, similarly constructed. 'Can you tell who the occupants were,' he asked. We stopped the car and looked at these two homes. No children around, only chickens . . . Chief says, 'Look at house number one, it has fruit trees, while house two has mielies growing around it. The first is an Indian home while the other is an African home. Indians cook and pickle the green fruit and eat them if any is left to ripen.' So it was, as the occupants came to check on the stationary car. [48]

Here Phyllis is being schooled in the complexities of race politics, in the divisions and contradictions in the ANC leadership that would have significant impact on the movement, and in the divergence of organized politics and daily life where racial segregation was concerned. Clearly an admirer of Luthuli, who won the Nobel Prize in 1961 and was assassinated in 1967, she recounts how she visited him at home when he was banned, and how Moses Kotane, Duma Nokwe and Govan Mbeki drafted his Nobel acceptance speech in her flat in Cross Street before bringing it to him in Groutville, where he lived while under the ban. The day the prize was announced, Naidoo was teaching English literature to a standard nine class at Durban Indian Girls' High School. Her students were silent when told of the honor. "Then a shy student said, 'You were not in Cato Manor when we hid in our ceilings and they burnt our homes in 1949.'"[49]

By invoking the Durban riots, this student cited what was already, by the early 1960s, a well-known, even a well-worn, narrative of Afro-Indian hostility that Naidoo's life's work has been dedicated to muting, if not subverting. Despite the vibrant mixture of communities in and around Victoria Street where the riots began, that narrative was perpetually in danger of being a spatially segregated one, and Naidoo's Luthuli stories interrupt it both by mapping "Indian Durban" as a mixed space where Indians and Africans could walk together—even when they were called out—and by recounting numerous other instances of joint political and social work across the color line as well. In the interior spaces of her flat and that of others, debates and strategizing took place, posters were made, enemies of the state were harbored and comrades black and brown fell asleep together, much to the distress of Phyllis' landlord.[50] In *Footprints* Phyllis is doing more than attempting to write a non-racial history; she's writing the non-racial history of the anti-apartheid struggle that *she* remembers living—its in-laws and its outlaws, to borrow an evocative phrase from Gomolemo Mokae's memoir of Robert McBride.[51]

This is not to say that she is without her critique of the race politics of the movement or, for that matter, of the ANC. Her embrace of Luthuli is itself a political act, as is her recounting of the meetings of the ANC they both attended, one in particular at Kathiwad Hall in Lorne Street, where they all sang Nkosi Sikelele. "As we stood up to sing... Dorrie Paton held on to my arm saying[,] if this is their strength when they sing, what will they be like if they fight for our freedom. I have always been so proud singing our anthem, that I was shocked by her fears." Positioned between white and black, Naidoo navigates a straight line that leaves no doubts as to her political commitments. "Chief has his footsteps firmly embedded in the Grey Street area and in all of South Africa." And the chorus: "Hamba Kahle Chief."[52]

Equally telling are Naidoo's chapters on Govan Mbeki and Jacob Zuma. Both accounts conjure the intense, almost breathless experience of underground militant politics of the 1960s and 1970s—offering detailed portraits of these young revolutionaries, their network of spies and runners and collaborators and above all, the footwork, sometimes quite fancy, of Naidoo and others in enabling their close escapes, money transfers and sub rosa lives. In Mbeki's story we hear how they walked the streets of Indian Durban together; what political lessons she learned from him; and that her father called him "a clever coon."[53] In Zuma's case, Naidoo offers a rare, self-consciously autobiographical take. "He is our Deputy President and my friend," she wrote at the time.

> I was his attorney on his release from Robben Island. But since I no longer practice law that relationship has gone overboard. If you wish to know his political profile, this is well documented in many books, ANC archives, internet, media. There is no dearth of material on him. With his engaging smile (not to be taken for granted) there is no shortage of media treatment of our Deputy President.
>
> What I have to say . . . does not figure in any of the above. In interviews he will probably not mention what follows, the details might vary, but what follows is indisputable. [54]

What follows is mainly an account of how Zuma managed after his release from Robben Island, a period of time when he was in need of work and subject to all the dompass laws that any other black South African was. Naidoo scotches a rumor that was apparently bruited about that he received his driver's license via corruption; in fact she goes into tremendous detail about how she helped him prepare, pay for lessons, etc. Perhaps the most remarkable feature of the Zuma chapter is the section, quite considerable in length, where he asks Naidoo to help the father of a Robben Island prisoner visit his son, Curnick Ndluvo. Curnick's father, whom Naidoo refers to as "Baba," turns up at her office and makes clear that he has nothing but contempt for her as woman and an Indian. "'Le Khula—(this coolie) do you think she will be able to arrange for me to see my son?' he asked of Zuma." If Zuma replied, Naidoo does not record it. She says, instead: "This is the English province of Natal and racism was not the preserve of the English. All Natalians were contaminated with this racist filth to a greater or lesser degree." She also notes, "I kept a straight face and shook his hand. He wore a pair of gumboots that he worked in. He was employed by the Durban Municipality in the fresh fish market in Warwick Avenue and had scrubbed the floor of the market before coming to see me. In the labour hierarchy he was at the bottom."[55]

Naidoo gets Baba travel clothes and money, arranges for his transport—the latter he refuses because it is offered by a Coloured woman, Toni Wilcox, in Cape Town, "who did not speak Zulu."[56] But he got to Robben Island. When he returns, Naidoo doesn't recognize him. His limp is gone, "his gait was certain... he did not shuffle along. He announced boldly that he was going to see the dockworkers on behalf of Curnick. He had to convey some messages before he went home." Naidoo's final word on Baba? "Yes! An activist is born! Thank you Toni! Thank you Zuma!" And in the end, Zuma leaves the country before his license is fully paid for (1975). Naidoo ends the chapter tantalizingly with this provocation: "He most certainly had an important skill in exile and a great story to tell if he had willing listeners." And in a direct address to one of her subjects himself, she says, "*Stay the caring human being I know you are, my friend and comrade.*"[57]

Like Cynthia in her law office, "Baba" is, for Naidoo, tangible evidence of the kind of grassroots politicization that interracial collaboration can produce. She cites him proudly, as an object of her tutelage and indeed, as a political accomplishment. Given what was unfolding in South Africa when she was writing *Footprints in Grey Street*—given indeed the whole history of African-Indian relations from the 1980s onward—such proofs are not politically innocent. Indeed, given the fate of Zuma governmentality in South Africa—a fate that even Naidoo could not reasonably have anticipated when she was writing *Footprints in Grey Street*—it's hard not to feel the immediacy of the unfolding post-apartheid present in this and indeed in all of Naidoo's auto/biographical entries.[58] Naidoo implicitly and explicitly rejects a break between 1994 and before, which I read in part as her refusal of the objectivity of History capital H. The political energy that gives *Footprints* its momentum derives from her conviction that the present needs more of the past, not less of it, specifically in the form of histories like the ones she recaptures—"small" histories that cite all the struggle workers and allow their work to be seen embodied in tragic, ordinary and exemplary ways.

Yet it would be a mistake to imagine that this is a pious or relentlessly serious book. Naidoo is capable of telling humorous as well as pedagogical tales. The text is peppered with poetry by the *Sunday Times* journalist Molly Reinhardt, who often "took up cudgels" on behalf of those who were banned or otherwise persecuted. Some of them are funny little ditties, like "Out of the Blue":

> *Twinkle twinkle little star*
> *How I wonder what you are*
> *Up above the world so high*
> *Like a diamond in the sky.*
>
> *Do not think I'm being tacit*
> *As I study every facet*
> *Understand my girlish fears . . .*
> *I prefer them from de Beers.*[59]

Beyond these witty insertions, Phyllis favors a good story that subverts the apartheid structure in all its ridiculous banality, especially if the story has a little scatology. In 1951 she lived in a room in a flat owned by Muthu Moodley and his wife Rajamath and their children in Wills Road. Muthu worked as a waiter in the Durban Club. One day Phyllis saw two pairs of underpants hanging up, which Muthu had brought home to be washed and ironed and had to take back to their owner the next day. Phyllis, who was quite amused by the size of the underpants, naturally wanted to know who their owner was. Muthu refused to reveal it.[60] Phyllis was determined, and he finally told her they belonged to the parliamentarian Sir Villiers Graaf. Winding us up for the punch line, Phyllis starts in on a history lecture:

> In the fifties, the Nats were riding rough shod over the Africans, creating homelands and new townships and Bantu Education; the Coloured lost their vote and Group Areas kicked them out of their homes; the Indians were stopped from trading and the Group Areas Act turfed us out far from the centre of town; the Communists were whacked out of existence; listing and banning orders spread its net overall; some newspapers were knocked out of existence—the whole caboodle that was apart hate....

When Muthu told her the underpants belonged to a Sir de Villers Graaf, she quipped:

> How close could a Black get to a white parliamentarian in the 50s?[61]

Even in jest, Phyllis does not lose an opportunity to identify Muthu as black, and thereby to link her Indian friend and landlord with the cause of non-racial solidarity.

Nor is Naidoo above making fun of the limits of her own racial knowledge. Charged with tending to the defendants' needs at the trial of Harry Gwala in the mid 1970s, she was given a task she could not quite get the gist of: she was asked by Zakhele Mdlalose to get them "GO BLACK." "'Can I get it at CNA,' [I asked], thinking it was a book. They all looked uncomfortably away. 'Is it a Black Consciousness book'" [she persisted]. 'No,' said Zak sheepishly. 'What is it and where will I get it?' I asked. All looked away, not knowing how to deal with me. Zak eventually says, it's hair dye. Ooops!"[62] The one she especially enjoyed telling was when she instructed someone in the CNR office to type letters she had drafted to be sent to Robben Island magistrates on behalf of prisoners. Her colleague was outraged to discover that in a slip of the tongue she had written, and the secretary had dutifully typed, "Dear Cur" instead of "Dear Sir."[63] As Thomas Blom Hansen has shown through his ethnographies of Chatsworth, such "jokework" is a common feature of the post-apartheid Indian cultural landscape —which suggests that the Indian public who might appreciate it is a crucial part of Naidoo's imagined audience for *Footprints*. As Hansen also suggests, that public—whose satirical traditions have a long history in South Africa—is both open and closed, endogamous but not neatly set off from other communities, especially in working-class contexts.[64]

In the end, despite the raucous fun these examples contain, it would be hard to gainsay the seriousness of Naidoo's purpose, especially given the fact that the deaths of her two sons and especially of Sahdhan's—assassinated in exile in 1989 in Lusaka along with Moss Mthunzi—loom so large over her life, her biography, and the autobiography of her own painful work in the struggle. In many ways, *Footprints* is a graveyard, strewn with the long dead, the recently dead, the presumed dead, the longed for dead. There are a few places in the first volume of the quartet where Naidoo asks, one might even say pleads with, the reader to help in the recovery of facts about specific individuals, and at least in one case, in the recovery of their killers and their bodies as well. In what starts as a humorous story about her son cursing on the toilet ends up in a story about an MK comrade, Sandy Jacobsen, whose death is a mystery and whose body remains to be found. "In this year 2002, the year of the Volunteer," Phyllis instructs, "ex MK comrades should volunteer their services to find the murderers of their comrades. You owe her that much."[65] In chapter called "Finding Godfrey Sekhukhene," Naidoo also seeks to bury the dead properly by filling out the stories of their lives. Godfrey was a male nurse in Zululand with a banned uncle to whom Phyllis is dispatched with a boot full of food on behalf of the Human Rights Committee (this trip involved a pregnant Naidoo crossing into territory from which she is legally precluded and being mistaken for the maid of the white couple with whom she drove). When they arrive they learn the uncle has died of starvation. As she writes her entry, she does not know where Godfrey is. "I wonder where you are in the new democratic SA?" she calls out to him.[66] For Naidoo, the struggle itself, the history of the antiapartheid movement is never done, and those in the present cannot read it as a thing of the past. Its open-endedness is what grabs at the reader, pulling us in and insisting that we be equally responsible for its denouement, even as we are called to resist its closure as politics.

If the vitality of struggle history is the mark of *Footprints*, it is equally the signature of Naidoo's, *156 Hands that Built South Africa*, published by Phyllis herself via Art Printers in Durban in 2006. A compendium of biographical sketches about the treason trialists of 1956, it is a frankly stunning piece of research and a labor of tremendous love. Naidoo's textual strategy is similar to the one she undertakes in *Footprints*, but it's matched by a complete photographic catalog that is moving beyond words.[67] Here too Naidoo is motivated by the unfinished business of anti-apartheid history, with a canniness about timing that is hard to gainsay: this volume was produced specifically for the 50th anniversary of 1956. Coming only four years after the publication of the first *Footprints* volume—incredibly—it exceeds that text in scope and scale. Her sketches are sketchier than in *Footprints*, and the photos are fuzzy: despite the high production value there are many fragmented accounts and many, many unanswered questions. Without a doubt, this text—with its evocation of powerful hands and minds and lives that built the struggle—is worthy of its own essay.

For now, and in conclusion, I must be content to treat it only briefly in comparison to *Footprints*, of which I have really only just scratched the surface as well. Less Durban-centered and more focused on the detention and very public trial of these 156 fighters, *156 Hands* looks and feels more like a textbook, a catechism addressed to an even broader South African public. She uses more stylized narrative forms; the text is not meandering, like a good walk down Grey Street, but all about the business of remembering the racist state. And yet Naidoo's informality is also in evidence. She directly addresses the reader, even scolds us, for our ignorance—in this instance, of "a world that put the Freedom Charter on trial and finally acquitted it on the

29th March 1961," when the last treasonist was released.⁶⁸ Her tone is angry and her history, more fervently directed at the contemporary regime. Her introduction ends with this cri de couer: "without the citizenship right what loyalty is owed to the state? No taxation without representation—you saw how we were forced into numerous taxes and were rendered criminals for non-payment. We paid for the instruments of our oppression." The contrast between then and now is palpable and painful. "'We Stand by Our Leaders' posters held by men and women appeared in the first weekend after the arrests on the 5 December," she recalls. "If 156 leaders were detained—Who carried on the struggle? Yes, who carried on the struggle?"⁶⁹ The repetition of that question underscores its double meaning, its interrogation of the past and for the present as well.

If *Footprints* is a kind of graveyard, *156 Hands that Built South Africa* is a more of a scrapbook, an impression derived mainly from the pictures that grace each entry and stare at us with varying degrees of forthrightness, shyness and defiance. The citations are as visual as they are textual; the text for each is more than a caption but also works in dialogic relationship to the image at hand. In part because of the photos, *156 Hands* can be seen as an attempt at a kind of pantheon of great, fallen leaders who defied the apartheid state—both by engaging in subversive activities and by surviving detainment and harassment and oppression. Again, it is a very mixed race collection, though the majority of entries here are of Africans (as the trialists were). As importantly, I think, in terms of the kind of anti-apartheid historical method Naidoo offers in *156 Hands*, the past is presented as usable in the present not only because it is a gadfly on contemporary memory and politics but because it is open-ended: in need of many details filled in, incomplete in terms of those details but also because of the narratives yet to be written that will be "built" from Phyllis' handiwork. Of Lungile Dickson Fuyani she asks: "where was he born? To whom? Did he have a family? Any children, who might have called him Dad?

Did he go to school? . . . was he arrested in the Defiance Campaign of 1952?"[70] Here, we see the historian openly at work. For the next page records a fax she's received from Fuyani via an intermediary (Raiza) that is an affadavit of sorts, testifying to his ANC membership, arrest, imprisonment. Elsewhere, she's less sanguine that the facts will ever be in; nor does she spare us her anguish at the knowledge that the task is beyond her capabilities. On Elmon Malele, "all resources are silent."[71] On Joshua Makue, even Doc's files are empty, though Phyllis is not one to believe in the totality of extant archives. "This does not mean he was not banned. Comrade Docrat may have missed him."[72] And she has scraps and scraps of evidence as well: "There is a single line describing David [H. Mgugunyeka] reading thus: 'born in 1906—commercial traveler. Prominent in the Defiance Campaign in Cape and Western Langa branch activities.'" The source is "the ANC publication—Unity in Action." [73] There's a recurrent humility tempered by exhaustion animating this book that reminds us that the clock is ticking—"my memory [is] in serious decline" she tells us in one of the last entries —that the refrain of Hamba Kahle is not just a salutation but a eulogy of what was and an elegy for what still might be.[74] In this sense, the rhythm of hands and feet is also a fateful, fitful chorus, chanting the fugitive histories yet to be nailed down, yet to be written, yet to be made full use of in contemporary history.

Let me end where I began, with Naidoo's signature management of the Indian/African question. The "I am not an Indian" declarative I opened with is not fanciful: it erupts in *Footprints* on the occasion of the birth of Cynthia Phakathi's daughter Ntobeko in hospital, at McCord's, in April 1977 after a very difficult, even life-threatening, labor. Naidoo and Judson Kuzwayo were both there. Was he the father? Phyllis does not say. She does recall Cynthia telling her that the nurses were "shocked" to see Phyllis at her bedside. "They had never seen an 'Indian' care for an African [Indian in quotes]. . . . They don't understand you. They don't understand that we are all

South Africans." Did Cynthia say this? Maybe yes, maybe no. That uncertainty, that interpretive lacuna, is part of the open ended-ness of Naidoo's history. What Naidoo herself does say on this occasion, in no uncertain terms, is that

> Both Cynthia and I are South Africans. I know no other home; my father was born here. My grandfather was brought from India to plant sugar cane here for the British in Natal ... I am not an Indian. I don't have an Indian Passport. If stranded anywhere the South African government and not the Indian government will come to my rescue. I don't want to be a South African of Indian origin. Nobody says a South African of British origin? I am a South African and very proud of it. [75]

The combination of defiance and intimacy, staged in this fraught hospital setting, reminds us what a queer subject Phyllis Naidoo is— by which I mean a subject who does not sit easily on any grid and in her uneasiness lays bare the wide spaces of possibility, defiance and desire between the slats.

I'm tempted to call *Footprints* an alternative archive, and it certainly does work to interrupt political pieties of the past and challenge their purchase in the present. But alternative does not mean disinterested; to the contrary. Phyllis is securing her own reputation in this set of very intimate political histories in the precincts of Indian Durban, and along its many margins as well. Mainly it's a recovery narrative, but there are some corrective moves too, at the level of specific incidents but at a meta-level as well: "the media demonized our struggle. All of us were terrorists. We were never people."[76] Introduced by Nobantu Mbeki, Govan Mbeki's grand-daughter, Naidoo intends *Footprints* to be a revisionist history and an *ubuntu* primer. Its ultimate address is to schoolchildren, whom she tells: "we have tried to make the cost of this book fit to your pockets ... I want you to read, to quote and know your glorious past."[77] Naidoo makes passionate use of the hands and feet of comrades black and white and coloured in this public service, in order to think and write as a "politico" who does not take a racially discrete view of South Africa for granted—to continue to try to work, in other words, as a freedom fighter who does not see a segregated history as inevitable either for Grey Street or its many splendored capillaries. Her vision is both aided and impeded by the verticalities of race: the story she tells is one of passion and patronage simultaneously. Her citationary impulse is affirmative of Afro-Asian/Afrindian histories in all their tense and tender moments; she rails against the fate of the footnote even as her citationary practices echo, at times, its vectors of power and positioning. Naidoo cannot, in other words, exceed the strictures of racial hierarchy that helped produce her as a historical subject, a political subject, even and perhaps most especially when she ardently aspires to do so. Given the complex material realties of life in South Africa before and after apartheid, it may be necessary to think non-racialism humbly, provisionally, aspirationally rather than as a fait accompli.

To do so is to think it problematically, which is what Naidoo's histories arguably try to do—in ways she is aware of and in ways she may not be. And here we must return to a scene she evokes when she tells the first of her stories of Cynthia's employment, cited above. I refer to the anecdote she related, almost in passing, about Robert Sobukwe calling her on the phone to seek legal aid from the joint partnership of Gumede and Naidoo. Let me reprise here:

> Archie was an African and I was of indentured Indian stock. But our common humanity outweighed any imposition by racists from wherever they came. I remember a call from Robert Sobukwe in Kimberley where he wanted help in a matter in the Durban Courts. He chose us for he found it strange that an Indian and African would be in a partnership in law. When I told him I suffered under restrictions similar to his, he dropped the phone on my ear.[78]

What could Naidoo have meant by this last comment, given Sobukwe's credentials as a critic of narrow, race-based African nationalism and as an advocate of the inclusion of Indian working class people, specifically in the context of the Pan Africanist Congress in 1959? Was her determination to have the shared struggle, sacrifice of Indians and Africans seem so powerful that she could not anticipate that some Africans might not be able to hear the challenge to solidarity in this particular racial context that was implied by her claim to equal suffering? Or, given the way knowledge did not flow so freely as it happened, or even after the fact, is it possible Naidoo was not privy to this information? Not least, what do we make of how she recorded his response (i.e., what did it mean that he dropped the phone on her ear)? I offer these questions in the open-ended spirit of Naidoo's own history-writing, in the hope that others will continue to take them up. Above all, how do we historicize the will to non-racialism and remain attentive to the contradictions and erasures at the site of racial inequality that shape that very impulse? How do we work and live with the limits of even alternative archives from which we desire to write counter-narrative histories?

For desire it is—the desire that animates all radical histories. If countenancing these questions remains a challenge for all aspirationally anti-racist histories—my own included—Naidoo is by no means alone in grappling with it, unwittingly or not. She walks the same pathway through anti-apartheid history as the photographer Omar Badsha, whose images cite the variety of entanglements in which Indians and Africans lived without necessarily embracing a strictly, or statically, racialized view of his subjects.[79] Taken together Naidoo and Badsha—comrades in the anti-apartheid struggle *and* chroniclers of Afrindian histories, both—raise the question of how we can do critical histories of a "non-racial" past when the apparatus we have available tends to relegate and (re)position as well as to sift and select and gloss in powerfully, if not inescapably, racial terms. Naidoo's work, the ferocity of her politics, also recalls that of other contemporary radical women in diaspora. In the spirit of the promise of "nonracial" citationary moves and unlooked for juxtapositions, and in an echo of my call in chapter 1 to re-think how we cite Singh's novel *Behold the Earth Mourns*, I reach here for Queen Mother Audley Moore, whose pan-African career and sensibilities resemble Naidoo's own commitments. Erik McDuffie has called Moore a "brilliant organic intellectual" and the same term readily applies to Naidoo.[80] If we cannot share Phyllis Naidoo's optimism or cope with her anger or count her "hands" and "feet" as a completely reliable archive, we can—we must—at least address her determination to leave an indelible impression on the future of anti-apartheid history-writing. It's an impression that, for all its flaws, must surely be reckoned with.

Notes

1. Tshque Harcharan, "Who Am I?" in Rob Pattman and Sultan Khan, eds., *Undressing Durban: Behind the Tourist Gaze* (Durban: Madiba Publishers, 2007), p. 370.

2. Aziz Hassim, *The Lotus People* (Johannesburg: STE, 2003), p. 511.

3. Quoted in Tejpal Ajji and Jon Soske, *South-South: Interruptions and Encounters* (Barnicke Gallery, Toronto, 2009), p. 11.

4. Phyllis Naidoo, *Footprints in Grey Street* (Durban: Ocean Jetty, 2002) and *156 Hands that Built South Africa* (Durban: Art Printers, 2006). All subsequent references are made to these editions.

5. The term is Pallavi Rastogi's: see her *Afrindian Fictions: Diaspora, Race and National Desire in South Africa* (Columbus: Ohio State University Press, 2008).

6. "'What political work did the Liberal Study Group do—or was it a talk shop?' I ask. Doc responds, 'We organized literacy classes and a library at Magazine Barracks. There was a dearth of schools with children over ten years not able to find accommodation. We campaigned for more schools. We assisted George Singh with organizing the Municipal Workers. If the mines paid two pounds then, you can imagine the role of the municipality. George Ponnen, Errol Shanley and H.A. Naidoo took up the dire oppression of sugar cane workers and their families. The Liberal Study Group opened the Gandhi Library to Africans. Sydney Smith an ex-mayor was very helpful'" (p. 51).

7   Ibid.

8   Ibid., p. 49.

9   Ibid., pp. 51–52.

10 Nelson Mandela, *Long Walk to Freedom* (Boston: Little Brown, 1994), pp. 102 and ff. Of the Indian-led passive resistance campaign he wrote, "the participation of other groups was not encouraged" (103). See also Ismail Meer, *A Fortunate Man* (Cape Town: Zebra Press, 2002), pp. 80–85.

11 Meer, *Fortunate Man*, p. 122. Meer earlier recalls AWG Champion of the ANC as rejecting the term African for himself in favor of "native" (p. 38).

12 See Sharad Chari, "The Antimonies of Political Evidence in Post-Apartheid Durban, South Africa," *Journal of the Royal Anthropological Institute* (N.S.) 2008: S74–75. Njabulo Ndebele, "Memory, Metaphor and the Triumph of Narrative," in Sarah Nuttall and Carli Coetzee, eds., *Negotiating the Past: The Making of Memory in South Africa* (Oxford: Oxford University Press, 1998), pp. 19–29.

13 Naidoo, *Footprints*, p. 171.

14 Ibid., p. 172.

15 Ibid., pp. 172–73.

16 Umkhonto we Sizwe (MK) was the armed wing of the African National Congress. For Naidoo see Phyllis Naidoo CV 1998 "Political Work: 1963–1977." BRN 1583, Gandhi-Luthuli Documentation Centre, UKZN-Westville (n.p). See also Tanya Lyons and Mark Israel, "Women, Resistance and the Armed Struggle in Southern Africa," in Pal Ahluwalia and Abebe Zegeye, eds., *African Identities: Contemporary Political and Social Challenges* (Surrey: Ashgate, 2002), pp. 42–50.

17 Ibid., p. 173.

18 By Naidoo's account this was sometime in 1977, right before Phyllis herself went into exile.

19 Ibid., p. 174.

20 Ibid., p. 175.

21 Ibid., p. 199.

22 Ibid., p. 40.

23 Lisa Lowe, "The Intimacies of Four Continents," in Ann L. Stoler, ed., *Haunted by Empire: Geographies of Intimacy in North American History* (Durham: Duke University Press, 2006), p. 207.

24 Nor was Durban the only "multicultural vortex" in South Africa. See Goolam Vahed and Thembisa Waetjen, eds., *Dear Ahmedbhai, Dear Zuleikhabehn: The Letters of Zuleikha Mayat and Ahmed Kathadra, 1979-1989* (Cape Town: Jacana, 2009), p. 3 and ff. Thanks to Kathy Oberdeck for putting this in my hands.

25 *Ibid.*, pp. 23-26.

26 For classic accounts of South African women's activism see Cherryl Walker, *Women and Resistance in South Africa* (London: Onyx Press, 1982) [for Indian women, pp. 111, 139) and Julia C. Wells, *We Now Demand! The History of Women's Resistance to Pass Laws in South Africa* (Johannesburg: Witwatersrand Press, 1993) [Indian women are not indexed].

27 *Ibid.*, p. 68.

28 Though Nyembe is not visible in the photographs for 1956 as far as I can see, she was one of the treason trialists. See Marie Human, Mothobi Mutloatse and Jacqui Masiza, eds., *The Women's Freedom March of 1956* (Johannesburg: Mutloatse Arts Heritage Trust, 2006), p. 119. Though she appears in Naidoo's *156 Hands that Built South Africa*, she is not in E.J. Verwey's *New Dictionary of South African Biography* (Pretoria: HSRC Publishers, 1995).

29 Iain Edwards, "Cato Manor, June 1959: Men, Women, Crowds, Violence, Politics and History" in Paul Maylam and Iain Edwards, eds., *The People's City: African Life in Twentieth Century Durban* (Pietermaritzburg: University of Natal Press, 1996), pp. 102-42; for urination story, see p. 131.

30 *Ibid.*, p. 69.

31 This is especially evident in the lengthy chapter on Mac Maharaj, which details the contents of what was seized in searches linked to him, the names of his interrogators and an extended memory piece from him as well (134-39). Phyllis has read his edited collection, *Reflection in Prison*, but she is determined to offer more detail here: "as you can see, there is much more to Mac" (*Footprints*, p. 132).

32 Naidoo also includes Nyembe in her *156 Hands that Built South Africa* and does quote her, but not on the subject of African-Indian relations. See *156 Hands that Built South Africa* (Durban: Phyllis Naidoo, via Art Printers in Durban 2006), pp. 154-55.

33 *Footprints.*, pp. 31–32.

34 *Ibid.*, p. 33.

35 *Ibid.*, pp. 18–19.

36 *Ibid.*, p. 19.

37 *Ibid.*, p. 32.

38 *Ibid.*, p. 19. By Naidoo's account, Lakhani Chambers at the corner of Saville and Grey Streets functioned as a similar hub. It was there that she met Florence Mkhize, "in Mr. Chetty's tailor shop" (p. 80).

39 Mandela, *Long Walk*, p. 148.

40 I am echoing George Lipsitz, *The Possessive Investment in Whiteness* (Philadelphia: Temple University Press, 2006). Fatima Meer's biography of Mandela, *Higher than Hope: The Authorized Biography of Nelson Mandela* (Hamish Hamilton, 1990), arguably exhibits this same investment. Conversely, Naidoo's *Footprints* does not give an entry to Chris Hani, for whom she was an MK comrade, a close confidante and a research subject as well. See Janet Smith and Beauregard Tromp, *Hani: A Life too Short* (Johannesburg: Jonathan Ball, 2009). Yet she did prodigious research and wrote a thirteen chapter biography of him; see Gandhi-Luthuli Documentation Centre archives, UKZN-Westville.

41 Naidoo, *Footprints.*, pp. 98–99.

42 It is an instructive counterpart to Manzi's own refusal to be interviewed for the ANC archive project, which Phyllis also notes in this chapter (p. 95).

43 See Andrew Lih, *The Wikipedia Revolution: How a Bunch of Nobodies Created the World's Greatest Revolution* (New York: Hyperion, 2009). For an interesting counterpoint, see Leslie Witz, "The Write Your Own History Project," in Joshua Brown et al., eds., *History from South Africa: Alternative Visions and Practices* (Philadelphia: Temple University Press, 1991), pp. 368–78

44 Naidoo, *Footprints,* p. 38, 82.

45 *Ibid.*, pp. 115–17.

46 *Ibid.*, p. 42.

47 For details on Naidoo's life, see http://overcomingapartheid.msu.edu/people.php?id=230; last accessed March 2011.

48 Naidoo, *Footprints.*, p. 28. See also Meer on Luthuli, *Fortunate Man*, p. 11 and p. 58.

49 *Ibid.*, p. 29. For a concise and compelling account of 1949 see Ashwin Desai, *Arise Ye Coolies: Apartheid and the Indian, 1960–1995* (Johannesburg: Impact Africa Publishing, 1996), pp. 9–14. For a firsthand account mediated by memory see Meer, *Fortunate Man*, pp. 116 and ff.

50 *Ibid.*, p. 133; see also p. 213.

51 Gomolemo Mokae, *Robert McBride—A Coloured Life* http://www.sahistory.org.za/pages/library-resources/online%20books/mcbride-robert/mcbride-index.htm—last accessed 11/12/10.

52 Naidoo, *Footprints*, p. 30.

53 *Ibid.*, p. 154.

54 *Ibid.*, p. 225.

55 *Ibid.*, p. 228.

56 *Ibid.*, p. 230.

57 Italics in the original.

58 For a sense of the present in which Naidoo was writing see Ashwin Desai, *We are the Poors: Community Struggles in Post-Apartheid South Africa* (New York: Monthly Review Press, 2002).

59 Naidoo, *Footprints*, p. 26.

60 *Ibid.*, p. 206.

61 *Ibid.*, p. 36.

62 *Ibid.*, p. 36.

63 *Ibid.*, p. 218.

64 Thomas Blom Hansen, "Melancholia of Freedom: Humor and Nostalgia among Indians in South Africa," *Modern Drama* 48,2 (2005): 297–315.

65 Naidoo, *Footprints*, p. 85.

66 *Ibid.*, p. 39.

67 In *Footprints* there are some photos in the back of the book, but they are by no means a full catalog of all the people she names chapters for. Those that

are missing have an image of footprints in place of an image. For a shorter, less ornamental list of the trialists see Anthony Sampson, *The Treason Cage: The Opposition on Trial in South Africa* (London: Heinemann, 1958).

68 Naidoo, *156 Hands*, p. 28.

69 *Ibid.*, p. 25.

70 *Ibid.*, p. 64.

71 *Ibid.*, p. 99.

72 *Ibid.*, p. 277.

73 *Ibid.*, p. 296.

74 The entry to which I refer is on Ebrahim Ismail Ebrahim and it is a reprint of two articles she's previously written on him rather than a "fresh" account (p. 238).

75 Naidoo, *Footprints*, p. 34.

76 *Ibid.*, pp. 140 and 13.

77 *Ibid.*, p. 16.

78 *Ibid.*, pp. 18–19.

79 Ajji and Soske, *South-South*, p. 53 and ff; see also Omar Badsha, *South Africa: The Cordoned Heart* (Cape Town: Gallery Press, 1986) and *Imperial Ghetto: Ways of Seeing in a South African City* (Cape Town: Kwela Books, 2006) and discussion of his work in Gerald Matt, Thomas Miesgang and Jyoti Mistry, eds., *Black, Brown, White: Photography from South Africa* (Wien: Kunsthalle, 2006). Ranjit Kally is their compatriot in this regard, and *Drum* an unparalleled archive; see Raison Naidoo, *The Indian in DRUM Magazine in the 1950s* (Cape Town: Bell-Roberts Publishing, 2008), pp. 124–25 (for Kally).

80 Erik S. McDuffie, "'I wanted a Communist philosophy, but I wanted us to have a chance to organize our people': the diasporic radicalism of Queen Mother Audley Moore and the origins of black power," *African and Black Diaspora: An International Journal*, 3, 2 (2010), 181–195.

Epilogue

> Did you know that our way of making tea is not original to us but comes from India?
> Kamiti, *Wizard of the Crow* (2007)

In Ngugi wa Thiong'o's 2007 novel, *Wizard of the Crow*, the hero Kamiti, university-educated and unemployed, poses as a wizard and topples a fictional African regime glutted on corruption and seduced by the evils of global capitalism. A marvelous feat of magical realism, Ngugi's novel sends up postcolonial despotism and Enlightenment rationality with characteristic wisdom, lyricism and wit. Among the things that make Kamiti who he is—i.e., what makes him a threat to the Republic of Aburiria and its would-be leaders—is that he has traveled through and studied in India. Just as irritating to his enemies is his praise for India's postcolonial accomplishments, his appreciation for the example of the Indian poor and his frank admiration of Gandhi as a political model. "...Wasn't it only after fifteen years of anticolonial struggles in South Africa that he went back to India to organize Satyagraha and ahimsa against British rule in India?" he asks Tajirika, here a prospective boss and later one of the many men in hot pursuit of him, as he tries to bring down the state through "sorcery."

'There is beauty in the man clad in calico sandals,' [Kamiti continued] 'armed with nothing but a walking stick and his creed of non-violence, taking on the might of the British empire, don't you think?'

'There now, you see my point?' Tajirika said. 'He lights a fire in South Africa and what does he do? Runs away when the going gets rough and leaves others to put it out or burn it. Young man, you have learned quite a bit of propaganda in India. So what else apart from Gandhi's propaganda and the Nehrus' monopoly of power did you learn?'

'Let's say I learned that there is not much difference between the political character of the Indian and the African" [Kamiti replied].[1]

If Kamiti is an avatar of the Africans in the writings I have been tracking—perversely figuring India as a challenge to the self-actualization of Africans' independence—he is also a critical marker of the persistence of Afro-Indian comparison in the postcolonial imagination.[2] Not just Gandhi but India and Indians are repeatedly cited by Kamiti as evidence of the path forward, and by his enemies as proof that he is not really African, or not purely so. His character and the structural interdependencies between India and Africa that it makes visible remind us that such citations are not simply a camera, taking snapshots of static relations of power. They are engines: motors of the tense, fractious, unsettling and ultimately political histories of race and its "machineries of knowing" that have shaped postcolonial history.[3]

As I hope is clear from the analyses I have undertaken in this book, my point in re-materializing some of this machinery, post-1945, is not to suggest that Indians were simply racists or did not participate in fighting apartheid in South Africa or in shaping Afro-Asian solidarity in the wake of the conference of non-aligned leaders at Bandung. The generations of South African Indians who succeeded Gandhi put their bodies on the line to protest racial segregation; and there is no gainsaying the impact of joint struggles by Indians and

Africans to secure a platform for Third World issues, and to re-world the postcolonial globe, in the heat of the Cold War and beyond. But accounts of the racial hierarchies at the heart of extra-India nationalism or extra-India political activity are not central to, or even actively cited in, diasporic historiographies, let alone in nationalist postcolonial ones. Nor is the question of sexuality—its linkages with racial hierarchy, caste politics and communitarian identity—as fully accounted for as it can and should be in these far-flung yet intimate histories. Indeed, what's telling about Kamiti's Indo-centrism is how connected it is with a kind of womanist/feminist solidarity that by his own account, enables him to partner both politically and romantically with the real wizard, Nyawira, *and* to effect a revolution of the sexual as well as the social order in Aburiria. In Ngugi's novel, the upending of gender hierarchies is among the most threatening aspects of the wizard's magic, not least because it's understood to be an import, coming from beyond the boundaries of the postcolonial nation. His Indo-philia makes Kamiti illegible as an African man and challenges the confraternities—the racialized normative order—at the heart of postcolonial nation-building in authoritarian regimes.

Ngugi is clearly having fun with these reversals, using satire and even farce to get at edgy and difficult questions with deep and vexed histories. Given the way that Indians appeared in his earlier novels— "as dirty-mouthed swindlers and petty capitalists" with a lascivious eye on African women—should we read this as a kind of "revisionary skepticism" about the purity of the postcolonial nation, as well as of his own citationary practices?[4] Ngugi's approach—one that is enviably open to him as a novelist—makes it impossible not to take the centrality of women and gender and sexuality in his story seriously as part of his critique of a certain species of postcolonial manhood in a global frame. Gender questions and feminist interpretive frameworks are alive in postcolonial historiography but they operate at a low frequency in contrast. And they have frankly failed to become indispensable to postcolonial method except by allusion or incorporation into "larger" paradigms and meta-narratives. Sex and race must be thought together in conjunction with class, caste and ethnicity not because they are dimensions of postcolonial history, but because they are at once symptoms and effects of its many-cited, multi-sited political frictions. Kamiti's Indian past offers, then, more than a mirror image of the political preoccupations of the writers I have considered here. Ngugi's fiction underscores the contemporaneity of the African/Indian question and the urgency of giving it truly embodied, deeply sedimented histories. Ideally, such histories will be more reciprocal than parallel, more conjunctive than discrete; more concerned with the lived experience of the hyphen by both Africans and Indians rather than simply with denaturalizing the racially endogamous world of Indians in and around Africa as I have tried to do here. They will be more affiliative, in short, but in ways that take up rather than erase tensions of race, class, sexuality and politics, in ways that privilege rather than disappear the frictions.[5] The kinds of feminist postcolonial histories I am calling for will do so without fixing such frictions as transhistorical, treating them instead as forces that collide in unlooked for ways with contingencies of time and particularities of place. And they will situate India in its multi-polar worldly contexts, right-sizing the India-Africa connection and its powerful, selective and ultimately unstable citationary apparatus alongside the variety of Indian postcolonial projects, internal and external that have been coincidental in historical time with it.[6]

In the end, citation is a technology that raises issues and in so doing, helps us to visualize how those issues have been framed.[7] It materializes symbolic and political economies that are not just aesthetic—the province of romance or melodrama—but ethical and always already politicized as well. As such it is riddled with tensions that, perforce, generate friction: the heat and light we need to make new histories. Hopefully, this study is a move in that direction.

Notes

1 Ngugi wa Thiong'o, *Wizard of the Crow* (New York: Anchor Books, 2007), p. 56.

2 As the young American PhD student in James Kilgore's recent novel observes with excitement, his supervisor shares his view that "Mugabe was destined to become the 'African Gandhi.'" *We are all Zimbabweans Now* (Cape Town: Umuzi, 2009), p. 48.

3 I draw here from Donald Mackenzie, *An Engine, Not a Camera: How Financial Models Shape Markets* (Cambridge: MIT Press, 2008); quote is from p. 12.

4 Elleke Boehmer, "Without the West: 1990s Southern Africa and Indian Woman Writers—A Conversation?" *African Studies* 58, 2 (1999): 157, 164.

5 I am grateful to Kamala Visweswaran, *Uncommon Cultures: Racism and the Rearticulation of Cultural Difference* (Durham: Duke University Press, 2010), pp. 12-14, for helping me think this through.

6 Kashmir might be a case in point; see Suvir Kaul, "Indian Empire (and the Case of Kashmir)," *Economic and Political Weekly* v. XLVI, no 13 (March 26, 2011): 66-75.

7 I draw here from David Campbell, "'Black Skin and Blood': Documentary Photography and Santu Mofokeng's Critique of the Visualization of Apartheid South Africa," *History and Theory* 48 (2009): 57 and Judith Butler: "a citation will be at once an interpretation of the norm and an occasion to expose the norm itself as a privileged institution." *Bodies That Matter* (New York: Routledge, 1993), p. 108.

Index

Adams, Tim, 16
Africa: aerial views of, 57, 58, 76 78, 79; British imperialism in, 65; caste in, 14; in civilizational hierarchy, 62, 65–66; Indian diaspora in, 54n23; Indian princes' interest in, 23n26; Indian settlers in, 62, 67, 68, 69; Indian travelers to, 64; Indian workers in, 23n25; labor pool of, 79; ocean world contact, 63; travelers' knowledge of, 64, 78. *See also* East Africa; tribalism, African
Africa, postcolonial: as decolonizing space, 59; as dependent of Asia, 61, 91; divisiveness in, 70; European access to, 77; failed-ness of, 59; First World universalism and, 61; former French territories, 62; global modernity in, 61; Indian awareness of, 14, 17; Indian responsibility for, 91; marginalization of, 71; Nehru's view of, 9, 92–93, 120n65; relationship to India, 1, 9–10, 14, 17, 22n21, 90, 91, 93; role in global south, 18; self-actualization of independence, 168; South Asian diaspora in, 12; Soviet internationalism in, 116; technical capabilities of, 92, 106, 113; trade with India, 93; vertical critiques of, 80. *See also* solidarity, Afro-Asian
African Americans: citationary practices concerning, 5; Dalits and, 15, 25n38, 78
Africanism, 67, 76

African National Congress (ANC): anti-pass law campaign, 48; Defiance Campaign (1950–52), 39; divisions in, 127, 147; Docrat in, 126–27; language of non-racialism, 52n3; P. Naidoo in, 146–47, 148; passive resistance of, 34; Umkhonto we Sizwe (MK) branch of, 130, 161n16; Youth League of, 39, 48
Africans: fitness for self-rule, 57; Gandhi's attitude toward, 10–11, 49
Africans, postcolonial: impact of India on, 100; youth assistance programs for, 92
African states: ethnography of, 57; nascent, 60; as objects of pedagogy, 61; progress in, 66; relationship to Indian state, 1, 12, 91; strongmen of, 66–67; universities of, 61
African students: Gandhi's, 13; in India, 90, 91, 92; Nehru's exhortation of, 120n65; political significance of, 116; in postcolonial India, 90, 91, 92, 93, 97, 109, 111; social/sexual contacts of, 93; in U.S., 116
African Students conference (Delhi, 1956), 114
Afro-Asian relationships: in anti-apartheid movement, 12, 133–34; in antiquity, 63; citationary apparatus of, 170; during Cold War, 17, 118n10; cross-racial affinities in, 66–67, 70; dominant narratives of, 17; feminist interpretations

of, 116–17; gendered, 113; historicized, 124; interdependence in, 168; lived experiences of, 170; photographic images of, 159; political activism in, 11–13; postcolonial, 8; pre-colonial, 6, 64, 81n14; racial confraternity in, 7; racial difference in, 7; redemptive, 2; sexual, 2–3, 93, 96–98; U.S. and, 5–6; vis-à-vis West, 25n37. *See also* solidarity, Afro-Asian; tensions, Afro-Asian
Ahmed, Sara, 4, 20; on vertical power relations, 19
airplane: as continentalizing technology, 76; energy of, 86n75; in Mau Mau uprising, 77
Allman, Jean, 74, 85n70
Ambalemba, Musa, 69
Amin, Idi, 17, 69
anti-apartheid movement: Afro-Asian endogamy of, 12; anti-pass law campaign, 135; brown-black frictions in, 145; cross-racial alliances in, 28, 124, 133–35, 137–38, 145, 146, 147; historical narratives of, 28; national narrative of, 145; non-racialism of, 127, 131, 133, 142, 148; open-endedness of, 153–54; passive resistance movement and, 32; people's history of, 132; political education in, 141; political histories of, 136; politics of, 27, 129; politics of citation in, 49; prison memoirs of, 136; rejection of difference, 145; South African Indians in, 8, 11, 28, 38, 168–69; women in, 26, 36, 128–32, 134–41
anti-colonialism, masculinist narratives of, 7
apartheid, South African: banality of, 151; end of, 25n39; Indian-African struggle against, 8, 11, 28, 38–39, 168–69; Jim Crow and, 15
Appadurai, Arjun, 5
Arenstein, Rowley, 129
Aryanism, civilizational difference in, 66
Asians, expulsion from Uganda, 17, 69

Asiatic Land Tenure and Indian Representation Bill (South Africa, 1946), protest against, 31
authors, African American: citationary practices of, 5

Badsha, Omar, 159
Baig, Tara Ali: *Portraits of an Era*, 75
Ballantyne, Tony, 66
Bandung Conference (Indonesia, 1955), 1–2, 21n13; African representatives at, 110; Afro-Asian solidarity following, 57–58, 91; and end of apartheid, 25n39; fraternal narratives of, 116; geopolitical concepts of, 92; legacy of, 7, 16; myth of, 6; Nehru at, 9–10; non-aligned leaders at, 168; in postcolonial histories, 7; racial confraternity at, 116; redemptive narratives of, 2; re-imagination of, 6–7; romance of, 12, 116; sodalities of, 76
Bhabha, Homi, 5
Bhatia, Prem, 69
bildungsromans: colonial, 90–91; postcolonial, 90, 97
biopower, technological, 104, 108
blackness: cultural capital of, 67; Indian distance from, 66; in postcolonial Indian imagination, 4, 5, 17, 112; in U.S., 5; Wright on, 85n70
"blood and nation," trope of, 16, 22n16
Boehmer, Elleke, 7
Bourke-White, Margaret, 75
British empire: core-periphery binary of, 62; effect of Indian independence on, 82n31. *See also* imperialism, British; Raj, British
brown: Indians as, 4; multiple meanings of, 20n5; racial superiority of, 18, 92
brown-black friendships, 3
Burton, Richard: *First Footsteps in East Africa*, 63
Butler, Judith: on citation, 171n7

capital relations, racialized, 2
Caribbean, Indian-African contact in, 24n31

Index ∞ 175

caste: in Africa, 14; African tribalism and, 69–71; civil rights communitarianism of, 6; feminist/queer account of, 21n8; link with race, 4, 103; in postcolonial history, 170; in satyagraha campaigns, 11; sexuality and, 169
Cato Manor (Durban, South Africa), women's demonstration in (1959), 135
Chakrabarty, Dipesh, 79
Chari, Sharad, 127
Chatterji, Suniti Kumar: *Africanism*, 64–65, 81n21; *India and Ethiopia From the Seventh Century BC*, 63–64; in *India-China Friendship Society*, 81n20; on Indian civilization, 65; racial prejudices of, 64–65
Chaturvedi, Benarasidas, 78
Chellaram (Indian trading company), 68
China, Afro-Asian solidarity and, 117n10
Chirwa, Vera, 74
Chou En Lai, 117n10
citation, politics of, 3–5, 76; in anti-apartheid narratives, 49; racializing, 8; reflexive accounts of, 80
citationary practices: across time, 79; African, 3–4, 12; concerning African Americans, 5; concerning India, 12; of decolonization, 8; of Indian-African connection, 170; of Indian histories, 10; modes of representation, 4; of postcolonial histories, 19–20; racializing, 4–5, 16; reproductive capacities of, 26n49; vertical, 4; visualization of issues through, 170
civilization, hierarchies in, 62, 65–66, 67
Coetzee, J.M., 80
Cold War: Afro-Asian relationships during, 17, 118n10; Afro-Asian solidarity during, 58; homosocial diplomacy of, 73–74; Indian identity in, 5; negritude in, 67; postcolonial history during, 2; postcolonial parameters of, 18
colonialism: "inferior"/ "superior" races in, 3; racial confraternity in, 76;

Ramayana, 23n27; surveillance state of, 59; violent response to, 111–12. *See also* imperialism, British
color, politics of, 13
Congo, Indian designs on, 94
conjugality, South Africa, 35–36, 51
conviviality, in transnational connections, 19
cooperation projects, Indian-African, 1, 22n21
Coovadia, Imraan: *High Low In-Between*, 51

Dalits, African Americans and, 15, 25n38, 78
David, Devadas Paul, 146
Daymond, M.J.: *Women Writing Africa*, 53n7
Deb, Harit Krishna, 63
decolonization: in Africa, 59; citationary practices of, 8; crises in, 59; fraternal connections in, 1; racial hierarchies of, 2, 4. *See also* postcolonialism
Demos, Abraham, 63
development, under imperialism, 112
development, postcolonial: African-Indian, 89, 90, 92–93, 97, 98, 112–14; histories of, 89; Indian rural, 106–9; Nehru's plans for, 89–90, 92–93; temporality of, 91; transnational, 89, 90; women in, 102, 114
Dhlomo, H.I.E.: "Valley of a Thousand Hills," 44, 55n37
diaspora: global narratives of, 15–16; historiographies of, 169; Indian-African encounters in, 15, 54n23; radical women in, 159; time/space frame of, 24n32; universal story of, 16
Dlamini, Stephen, 130
Dlomo, Albert, 134
Dlomo, Bongi: activism of, 134
Docrat, Abdul Khalik Mohamed: activism of, 125–27; archives of, 126, 156; education of, 126; in Liberal Study Group, 125, 160n6; non-racialism of, 126–27
Doke, Joseph J., 56n43

Drum (South African newspaper), 28, 165n79
Dube, John, 11
Durban (South Africa): Afro-Asian community of, 123–24; Afro-Asian relationships in, 4, 11; Afro-Indian hostility in, 147; cosmopolitanism of, 11; Indian merchant community of, 36; Lakhani Chambers, 146, 163n38; mixed spaces of, 147; riots of 1949, 41, 147, 164n49; South Asian diaspora in, 12; World Cup in, 29, 50. *See also* Grey Street (Durban, South Africa)

East Africa: Afro-Indian tensions in, 69, 83n38; Indian interest in, 10, 23n26, 68; Ismaili community of, 68
East African Indian National Congress (EAINC), on Tanganyika, 10
Ebrahim, Ebrahim Ismail, 165n74
Edwards, Iain, 135
Essop, Hassan, 36
Esty, Jed, 90
Ethiopia, Indian soldiers in, 64
Europe, provincialization of, 79
exceptionalism, Indian, 70

Farred, Grant, 80
Ferguson, James, 19
First, Ruth, 130
FOSA (Friends of the Sick Association, South Africa), 128
Freund, Bill, 24n30
Furtado, Aquino: *Cidades Africanas*, 85n69
Fuyani, Lungile Dickson, 155–56

Gandhi, Mohandas: African students of, 13; Afro-Asian citations of, 6; anti-imperial campaigns of, 94; attitude toward Africans, 10–11, 49; non-violence manifesto in, 34; as political model, 167–68; prison memoirs of, 55n28; protest of Asiatic Land Tenure Act, 31–32; satyagraha campaigns of, 11, 34, 36, 167; in South Africa, 10–11, 32, 56n47, 168–69
Geiger, Susan, 74
gender: in global politics, 18; in racial thinking, 74; in satyagraha campaigns, 36; South African Indian ideals of, 38; verticalities of, 74
geopolitics: of Bandung Conference, 92; Nehru's, 10; postcolonial, 8; of resistance, 132
Ghana, effect of Indian independence on, 82n31
Ghetto Act. *See* Asiatic Land Tenure and Indian Representation Bill
Ghosh, Amitav, 79; *Sea of Poppies*, 17
globalization: non-national, 16; politics of, 18; south-south, 1
Godlberg, Denis, 133
Goswami, Manu, 89
Govinden, Devarakshanam, 29, 38, 49
Graaf, Sir Villiers, 151–52
Grey Street (Durban, South Africa), 123; Africans in, 134; anti-apartheid history of, 144; class-based solidarity of, 144; imaginative precincts of, 141; as metaphor, 144; in South Africa history, 145. *See also* Naidoo, Phyllis: *Footprints in Grey Street*
Guevara, Che, 131
Gumede, Archie J.: partnership with Naidoo, 137–38, 139–41, 142, 158
Gunther, John: *Inside Africa*, 73
Gupta, Dhruba, 115
Gurnah, Abdulrazak: *Desertion*, 17
Gwala, Harry, 152

Habshis, in India, 13, 63–64
Hall, Kim: *Things of Darkness*, 120n57
Hall, Stuart, 16
Hani, Chris, 163n40
Hansen, Thomas Bom, 15, 152
Hassim, Aziz: *The Lotus People*, 123
Hawley, John, 25n37
Hinduism, secularism and, 96

histories, Indian: citationary practices of, 10; postcolonial, 16
histories, postcolonial: Afro-Asian solidarity in, 19, 79; caste in, 170; celebratory narratives of, 20; citationary apparatus of, 19–20; feminist, 19–20; in fiction, 17; gender questions in, 169; Indian, 16; of Indian development, 89; meta-narratives of, 170; race in, 168; sexuality in, 170
histories, South African: counter-narratives, 159; de-segregation of, 145; Grey Street in, 145; resistance in, 132
Hoad, Peter, 17
Hofmeyr, Isabel: on Bandung Conference, 7; on *Behold the Earth Mourns*, 54n23
homeland, shifting meanings of, 56n45
homosociality, of Cold War politics, 74, 76
Horne, Gerald, 6
human rights, universal, 28

iconography, colonialist, 26n49
identity, African: relationship to Indian identity, 50
identity, Indian: Africanization of, 18; bourgeois cosmopolitan, 95–96; coherence of, 3; in Cold War, 5; gendered, 92; modern, 21n8; politics of, 29, 144; postcolonial, 14, 18, 50, 65, 66, 71, 92; racialized, 14, 27–28, 34, 43, 47–48, 49, 71; relationship to African identity, 50; sexual difference in, 14; in South Africa, 27–28
Ilanga Lase Natal (newspaper), 28
imperialism, British: in Africa, 65; civilizational hierarchy of, 67; history of, 25n36; India-over-Africa ethos of, 9; legacy of, 14; racializing apparatus of, 14; remnants in Africa, 61–63; verticality of, 62, 66. *See also* British Empire; colonialism; Raj, British
indentured laborers, Indian: centenary in South Africa, 48, 49; in Natal, 29; taxation of, 36; travel viewpoints of, 86n76

India: Africans in, 13; as allegory of colonialism, 83n32; British imperial views of, 62; in civilizational hierarchy, 65–66, 67; developmentalist narratives of, 18; labor pool of, 79; merchant travelers from, 64; as referent for Africa, 70
India, postcolonial: African students in, 90, 91, 92, 93, 97, 109, 111; Africa policy of, 1, 9–10, 22n21; Africa's role in, 14, 93; asymmetry with Africa, 12; colonial ambitions of, 10, 23n26, 68, 94; contrast with Japan, 72; dependence on African markets, 93; designs on East Africa, 10, 23n26, 68; domestic underdevelopment in, 107; educational projects of, 90, 91, 101, 102; geopolitical reeducation in, 90; in global marketplace, 89; imaginaries of, 3, 4, 5, 10, 17, 112; impact on visiting Africans, 100; imperial continuity in, 65; languages of, 70; leadership of Asia, 60; misogyny in, 105, 107; modernization programs of, 89–90; nationalist heterosexual couple in, 96; neo-colonial power of, 93; normative conjugality in, 104; "outreach" to Africa, 90; patriarchy in, 35–36, 105, 107, 114; perspective on Africa, 59–61; racial politics of, 13, 18, 90; *realpolitik* of, 110; relationship to Africa, 1, 9–10, 14, 17, 22n21, 90, 91, 93; responsibility for Africa, 91; rural community development in, 106–9; sexual politics of, 18, 90; technological improvement in, 108; unity in diversity of, 94
Indian Ocean: cosmopolitanism of, 131; racial taxonomies of, 76; South Asians on, 18
Indians: diaspora in Africa, 54n23; distance from blackness, 66; of Nairobi, 10; racial diversity of, 20n5; relationship with Britons, 8; settlers in Africa, 62, 67, 68, 69. *See also* women, Indian
Indians, colonial-born: activism of, 32; imperial citizenship of, 66

178 ⁓ Index

Indians, postcolonial: awareness of Africa, 14; bourgeois cosmopolitanism, 91; as consumers of Africa, 13–14; view of Africans, 98

Indians, South African: anti-apartheid activism of, 8, 11, 28, 38, 168–69; class/caste tensions among, 32; collective identity of, 51; conjugal choices of, 35–37; family life of, 35, 36; gender ideals of, 38; imperial prestige of, 54n23; indentured laborers, 29, 48, 49; middle-class, 144; in passive resistance movement, 28; political commitment of, 144; property rights of, 31; racial discrimination against, 27, 31, 39; settler identity of, 27, 30; state regulation of, 35; successors of Gandhi, 168

Jacobsen, Sandy, 153
Janira (Habshi state), 64

Kally, Ranjit, 165n79
Kaplan, Martha, 15, 19
Kashmir: Indian designs on, 94; postcolonial projects in, 171n6
Kelly, John D., 15, 19
Kennedy, Robert F., 77; Day of Affirmation Speech (South Africa, 1966), 76
Kenya: emulation of India, 114; nationalism in, 101, 114
Kenyatta, Jomo, 66; *Facing Mount Kenya*, 67; trial of, 9
Kilgore, James: *We are all Zimbabweans Now*, 171n2
Kotane, Moses, 147
Kramer, Paul, 116
Kroonstad prison, anti-apartheid activists in, 135–36
Kuzwayo, Judson Diza, 144, 156

Lee, Christopher J., 6
Liberal Study Group (Durban, South Africa), 125, 160n6
Lipsitz, George, 163n40

literature, juxtaposition with politics, 51–52
Loomba, Ania, 70–71
Lowe, Lisa, 133
Luthuli, Chief Albert, 146–47, 148; Nobel Prize of, 147

Maharaj, Mac: *Reflection in Prison*, 162n31
Makhoba family, 134
Makue, Joshue, 156
Malele, Elmon, 156
Mandela, Nelson, 76; African exclusionism of, 127, 161n10; law practice of, 141–42; on passive resistance campaign, 161n10
Mani, Lata, 35
Manzi, Gladys, 142–43, 163n42
Maphumulo, Shadrack, 130
Markham, Charles, 68–69
marriage, South African: restrictions on, 35, 45; Searle decision on, 36
masculinity: African, 94, 110–11, 115; postcolonial, 9
Matusevich, Maxim, 116
Mau Mau uprising, 68; airplane in, 78; atrocities of, 9, 77
Mbeki, Govan, 147, 148
Mbeki, Nobantu, 157
McDuffie, Erik S., 160, 165n80
McGill University, Indian Ocean World Centre, 8
Mdlalose, Zakhele, 152
Meer, Fatima: biography of Mandela, 163n40
Meer, Ismail, 11, 55n37, 161n11; on Mandela, 127
Mgugunyeka, David H., 156
miscegenation, 75; Indian fear of, 18, 92, 113
misogyny, in postcolonial India, 105, 107
Mitchell, Philip, 62
Mkhize, Florence, 163n38
modernity, Indian postcolonial, 89–90, 91–92, 112
Mongia, Radhika, 36, 37, 38
Moodley, Muthu, 151–52

Moodley, Poomoney, 128–32, 136; death of, 131; detention of, 129, 130; early life of, 128; ill-health of, 128, 129; interracial credentials of, 130; memory of, 130–31; in Umkhonto we Sizwe (MK), 130
Moodley, Subbiah, 132–33
Moore, Queen Mother Audley, 160, 165n80
Moraes, Beryl, 75
Moraes, Dom: *My Father's Son*, 75
Moraes, Frank, 3, 10; African diary of, 74, 85n64; as Cold War expert, 59; and Gunther, 73; journalism career of, 58; marriage to Beryl Moraes, 75; and Naipaul, 79, 86n81; relationships with women, 75; travels in Africa, 58, 64, 68
—*The Importance of Being Black*, 12; above-below perspective of, 58–60, 61, 65, 66, 68, 71–72, 76–77, 80; aerial view of, 57, 58, 77, 78; African chauvinism in, 72; Africanism of, 76; African nationalism in, 68; African strongmen in, 66–67; African women in, 74, 75–76; Asian perspective of, 59–61, 76; "Asian problem" in, 68–69; audience of, 71, 72; British imperialism in, 61–63; caste in, 69–71; citationary practice of, 58; civilizational hierarchy in, 65, 66, 67; Cold War politics in, 59; East Africa in, 68; emergent states in, 59; essay version of, 72; ethnography of, 61; gendered hierarchies in, 58; genealogies of the present in, 59; imperial past in, 62–63; imperial racial language of, 74; Ismaili community in, 68; Kenya in, 68–69; Kenyatta in, 66, 67; on negritude, 71; Nehruvian state in, 60; Nkrumah in, 66, 67; Nyerere in, 66, 67–68; political focus of, 72–73; politics of citation in, 76; progressive moments in, 71; publication of, 71; racial formation in, 71; racial views of, 66, 76; reception of, 72–73, 76; South Africa in, 80n3; timeliness of, 73, 84n58; travelogue mannerisms in, 72; tribalism in, 69–70; US readers of, 72;

verticality of, 57, 77; and Wright's *Black Power*, 85n70
—*India Today*, 81n13
—*Introduction to India*, 81n13
—*Witness to an Era*, 75
Morrison, Tony: *Playing in the Dark*, 29
Mthunzi, Moss, 153

Naicker, George, 141
Naidoo, H.A., 160n6
Naidoo, K.G. (Dr. Goonam), 33–34, 37
Naidoo, Phyllis, 3, 10, 19; in ANC, 146–47, 148; anti-apartheid activism of, 137; anti-apartheid histories of, 159–60; biography of Hani, 163n40); black prejudice against, 149; careers of, 124; children of, 138; citationary practices of, 4, 124, 145, 158; contribution to anti-apartheid history, 145; cross-racial associations of, 139–40; death of sons, 153; exile of, 131, 142, 161n18; family of birth, 146; Grey Street quartet of, 124, 132; historical sensibility of, 131; Indian identity of, 17–18; investment in blackness, 142; law practice of, 137–42, 149–50, 158; linguistic knowledge of, 132; at Non-European Section of Natal University, 146; non-racial politics of, 124; optimism of, 160; political education of, 145–48; political life of, 132, 135, 158; racial knowledge of, 152; racial politics of, 145; South African identity of, 123; teaching career of, 147; in Umkhonto we Sizwe (MK), 130
—*Footprints in Grey Street*, 13, 124; Afrindian solidarity in, 136, 137, 139–40, 142, 156; Afro-Indian relationships in, 133–34; as alternative archive, 157; audience of, 143–44; autobiographical voice of, 146, 150; biographies of, 125, 132–34, 145–46; citationary practice of, 127–28, 137; class-based solidarity in, 144; commemoration of the dead in, 153; cross-racial alliances in, 134–35, 137–38,

150, 159; Cynthia Phakathi in, 137–42, 156; Docrat in, 125–27; farewells in, 131–32, 136; Grey Street inhabitants in, 130, 133, 134; Gumede in, 138, 139–41, 142, 158; Hamba Kahle in, 131; humor in, 151–53; imagined audience for, 152; invisible histories of, 136–37; Luthuli in, 146–47, 148; Manzi in, 142–43; Moodley in, 128–32; motherhood in, 137–39; narratives of affirmation in, 133–34; non-racialism of, 127, 131, 133, 142, 148; Nyembe in, 135–37; open ended-ness of, 157; political education in, 143–44; readers' education, 143–44; realism of, 127; as recovery narrative, 157; revisionist history of, 157; scatology in, 151–52; scope of, 132–33; struggle in, 126, 128, 132, 134, 136, 142–43, 144, 150, 154; as *ubutu* primer, 157; women's alliances in, 134–35; Zuma in, 148–50
—*156 Hands that Built South Africa*, 124, 162n28,162n32; anti-apartheid method in, 155; citations of, 155; "Hamba Kahle" in, 156; photographs of, 154, 155; textual strategy of, 154; treason trialists in, 154–56
Naidoo, Sahdhan, 153
Naidu, Sarojini, 10, 23n25
Naipaul, V.S.: in East Africa, 86n81; marriage of, 86n81; view of Africa, 79–80
Naoroji, Dadabhai, 66
Natal: Indian indentured laborers in, 29; violence in, 136
Natal Indian Congress, Passive Resistance Council, 32
nationalism: extra-Indian, 169; postcolonial, 7; role of color in, 72
nationalism, African, 62; Kenyan, 101, 114; negritude in, 68; race-based, 158
nationalism, Indian: methodological, 89
Nazareth, Peter: *In a Brown Mantle*, 17
Ndebele, Njabulo, 127
Ndluvo, Curnick: father of, 149, 150

Nehru, Jawaharlal: African development projects of, 92–93; on Africans, 110; Afro-Asian citations of, 6; and Afro-Asian solidarity, 9–10; at Bandung Conference, 9–10, 110; contemporaries' views of, 23n24; development under, 89–90; exhortation of African students, 120n65; geopolitics of, 10; on Indian diaspora, 54n23; non-alignment policy of, 72
Ngugi wa Thiong'o, gender hierarchies of, 169
—*Wizard of the Crow*, 167–70; African/Indian question in, 170; citationary practices of, 169; Indo-centrism of, 169; magic realism of, 167; postcolonial manhood in, 169
Nkrumah, Kwame, 66, 67; release from prison, 82n31
Nokwe, Duma, 147
nonalignment, Afro-Asian, 1
non-racialism: of African National Congress, 52n3; of anti-apartheid movement, 127, 131, 133, 142, 148; Docrat's, 126–27; in South African politics, 124, 127; will to, 159. *See also* racialism
non-violence, Gandhian, 34; in *The Morning After*, 94, 98, 101, 112, 114. *See also* passive resistance movements; satyagraha campaigns
Nyembe, Dorothy, 135–36, 137, 162n32; among treason trialists, 162n28
Nyerere, Julius, 66, 68, 82n31; view of Indians, 67–68

Oliver, Roland, 72–73
Organize or Starve (SACTU history), 144

Pan Africanist Congress (1959), 158
panchayat, Indian: African tribal councils and, 70, 72
Pandit, Vijay Lakshmi, 12
Pankhurst, Sylvia and Richard, 63

Passive Resistance Campaign (South Africa, 1946–48), 12, 28, 37, 41, 48, 56n43, 127; Mandela on, 161n10
passive resistance movements: of African National Congress, 34; South African Indians in, 28. *See also* non-violence, Gandhian; satyagraha campaigns
Patel, Zubeida, 141–42
Paton, Dorrie, 148
Paul, Annie, 124
Phakathi, Cynthia, 137–42, 156; child of, 138
Phakathi, Ntobeko, 156
Pillay, T.V.R., 132
Pillay, Lake Rajaluxmi, 132
politics: juxtaposition with literature, 51–52. *See also* racial politics; sexual politics
politics, cross-racial: hidden histories of, 50
politics, global: feminist scholars on, 18
politics, postcolonial: global frame of, 2; racial categories of, 5, 116; sexual politics in, 117; triumphalist, 7
politics, South African: of conjugality, 35–36, 51; non-racial, 124, 127; racial, 28; struggle, 126; upward mobility in, 128
Ponnen, George, 160n6
postcolonialism: aerial views of, 79, 86n79; Afro-Indian comparison in, 168; colonial tropes in, 80; contact zones of, 90, 116; crises in, 59; as historical condition, 79–80; versus postimperialism, 14; racial confraternity in, 76; racial difference in, 7, 14, 15; racial hierarchies of, 2, 4, 9; racialized order of, 3, 8, 169; redemption narratives of, 8; U.N., 12; universal story of, 16; U.S. role in, 15. *See also* Africa, postcolonial; decolonization; India, postcolonial; politics, postcolonial
postcolonial states: bottom-up creation of, 61; racial logics of, 6–7
postcolonial studies: transnational connections of, 19; west/non-west in, 25n38

power relations: dynamism of, 4–5; vertical, 19, 110
Puar, Jasbir, 19

race: in African/Indian literature, 17–18; as analytical category, 5; civil rights communitarianism of, 6; global narratives of, 15–16; hierarchies of, 2, 4, 9, 42, 158, 169; link with caste, 4, 103; material production of, 16; political histories of, 168; political power of, 50; in postcolonialism, 5, 168, 170; in satyagraha campaigns, 11; in South Asian histories, 79; symbolic production of, 16; U.S.-centric discourse of, 15
racial formation: in Indian identity, 71; South African, 30; U.S., 5, 6; western, 15
racialism: in Afro-Asian solidarity, 90; of British imperial apparatus, 14; in capital relations, 2; in citationary practices, 4–5, 16; in Indian identity, 27–28, 34, 43, 47–48, 49; in politics of citation, 8; of postcolonial politics, 116; romance of, 116. *See also* non-racialism
racial politics: of *Behold the Earth Mourns*, 29, 30; postcolonial, 5; of postcolonial India, 18, 90; South African, 28; south-south, 8–9
Raj, British: racial confraternity of, 76; subimperial status of, 76
Rama Rau, Santha, 9; public life of, 84n60
Ramphele, Mamphela: *Across Boundaries*, 51
Ramusack, Barbara, 23n26
Rastogi, Pallavi, 160n5
resistance: geopolitical imaginary of, 132; global history of, 14
Robben Island: families of prisoners, 143; magistrates of, 152; prisoners of, 28, 134, 139, 141, 149–50
Roux, Eddie: *Time Longer than Rope*, 144
Roy, Srirupa, 82n22

SACTU (South African Trades Union), 128, 135; history of, 144
Saldana-Portillo, Maria Josefina, 7
Salih, Tayeb: *Season of Migration to the North*, 120n66
Sapru, Tej Bahadur, 69
Satapatha-Brahmana, dating of, 63
satyagraha campaigns: in *Behold the Earth Mourns*, 31–39; conjugal aspects of, 48; Gandhi's, 11, 34, 36; gender issues in, 36; merchant capitalist interests in, 33; race/caste in, 11; in Transvaal, 11. *See also* non-violence, Gandhian; passive resistance movements
Schueller, Mailini Johar, 5
secularism, Hinduism and, 96
Seedat, Dawood, 129
Sekhukhene, Godfrey, 153
Sen, Amartya: *The Argumentative Indian*, 83n42
Sen, Chanakya (Bhabani Sen Gupta), 3, 10, 117n1
—*The Morning After*, 13, 63, 102–3; African alienation in, 101; African characters of, 94, 110–15; African masculinity in, 94, 110–11, 115; African students in, 93, 97, 109, 111; African womanhood in, 111; Afro-Asian solidarity in, 91, 98–99, 101, 109, 111, 112, 115; Afro-Indian intimacies in, 90, 93–95, 97–107, 109, 110–11, 113, 114; anglophilia in, 96; Bengali version of, 90, 113, 115; black colonial subjects in, 107; bourgeois cosmopolitanism in, 95–96, 106; caste in, 103; citationary apparatus of, 113; class status in, 104; development in, 93–94, 98, 104, 105–9, 112–14; English version of, 115; family in, 94–97, 102–3; female heterosexual desire in, 104; Gandhian non-violence in, 94, 98, 101, 112, 114; gender politics of, 105; Indian home in, 93; Indian identity in, 95; marriage in, 102–4; misogyny in, 105, 107; modernizing universal subject of,

92; patriarchy in, 105; political education in, 110; in post-Bandung history, 115; as postcolonial bildungsroman, 90, 97; postcolonial bureaucracy in, 96; postcolonial cosmopolitanism in, 94; postcolonial modernity in, 112; racial dynamics of, 100, 112; racist anxiety in, 94–95; tropes of blackness in, 112; upward mobility in, 104
sexuality: caste and, 169; in global politics, 18; Indian women's, 96; interracial, 2–3, 76, 91; postcolonial, 15; in postcolonial history, 170; racial hierarchy and, 169; in racial thinking, 74
sexual politics: postcolonial, 117; of postcolonial India, 18, 90; south-south, 8–9
Shanley, Errol, 160n6
Sharpeville Massacre (1960), 48
Sidis, in India, 13
Silverstone, Marilyn, 74–75
Singh, Ansuyah R., 3, 10; activism of, 37; Afro-Asian relationships in, 12; liberal feminism of, 38; medical practice of, 37
—"Antenatal Stress and the Baby's Development," 37
—*Behold the Earth Mourns*, 12, 28–52, 143; African characters of, 29–30, 39, 40–46, 48, 49; African/Indian interactions in, 29, 30, 31; anti-apartheid struggle in, 28–29, 39; citational strategies of, 29, 30, 159–60; citation of, 49–50, 51; class difference in, 45; colonial power in, 32; family in, 38, 39; feminist reading of, 30; as heritage history, 39; historical significance of, 48, 51; horizontal reading of, 48; idealism/realism in, 41, 44, 46; incarceration in, 42, 43; Indian identity in, 30; Indian marriage plot of, 31–39, 45; as Indian national literature, 49–50; Indian women in, 36, 37–38, 43, 45–47; interracial engagement in, 30, 41, 42–47, 48; interracial reading of, 50–51; jacket

Index ○ 183

of, 53n6; Mayibuye Afrika in, 39–48; Passive Resistance Campaign (1946–48) in, 37–38, 41, 42, 48, 54n23; passive resistance in, 29; political education in, 34, 39–40, 42, 43, 45, 46; as political memoir, 51; politics of, 38; politics of identity in, 29; property rights in, 32; racial hierarchy in, 42; racialized identity in, 34, 43, 47–48; racialized topography of, 29; racial politics of, 29, 30, 50; racist legislation in, 37; as reclamation project, 38; recovery agenda of, 29; resistance in, 36; satyagraha in, 31–39, 43, 54n23; sovereign subjects of, 43; structure of, 46; as struggle literature, 30, 39; twenty-first-century reading of, 51, 52; as utopian novel, 38
Singh, Ganga (maharaja of Bikaner), 23n26
Singh, George, 160n6
Sinha, Subir, 108
Slovo, Gillian: *Every Secret Thing*, 51
Smith, Sydney, 160n6
Sobukwe, Robert, 140, 158
solidarity: Asian-Western, 71; south-south, 57, 79, 108
solidarity, Afro-Asian, 1–2; China and, 117n10; during Cold War, 58; competing statuses in, 19; conviviality in, 19; development projects of, 89, 90, 98; education projects in, 90, 91, 101, 102; extra-national spaces of, 19; fictive discourse of, 76; following Bandung Conference, 3, 57–58; gender politics of, 113–14; histories of, 48–49; homosociality of, 105–6; Indian leadership in, 92; in Indian postcolonial theory, 79; Indian self-interest in, 108–9; interracial intimacies in, 90, 93, 94–95, 97–107, 109, 110–11, 113, 114; interracial sexuality in, 96–98; male domination of, 114; mimicking of imperial power, 114; Nehruvian state and, 9–10, 60, 76, 95; in postcolonial histories, 19; pre-colonial, 64; racial dynamics of, 100; racialism in, 90; redistributive justice in, 108; romance of, 112; scholarship on, 10; sentimentalized history of, 20; in South Africa, 12–13, 41, 50, 55n31; structural conditions of, 106; technological transfer in, 106, 113; in Third World issues, 168–69; unravelling of, 115. *See also* Afro-Asian relationships
Soske, Jon, 11, 83n32; on African intellectuals, 67; on ANC, 52n3
South Africa: African labor in, 125, 126; Afro-Asian relationships in, 4, 10–12, 28, 52n3; Afro-Asian solidarity in, 12–13, 41, 50, 55n31; anti-Indian legislation in, 31–32, 33, 35, 37, 39; ban on cross-racial alliances, 46; citizenship rights in, 155; Doctor's Pact, 127; feminist scholars on, 48; Freedom Charter of, 126; Freedom Fighters of, 142–43; Gandhian legacy in, 11; gendered political struggle of, 48; Indian question in, 126; National Party government, 31; non-Christian marriage in, 36; Passive Resistance Campaign (1946–48) in, 12, 28, 37, 41, 48, 56n43, 127, 161n10; politics of conjugality in, 35–36, 51; post-apartheid present of, 150; prison life in, 51; racial formation in, 30; racial identity in, 48; satirical traditions of, 152–53; State of Emergency, 125; township system of, 47; treason trialists, 154–56, 162n28, 165n67; during World War II, 125. *See also* anti-apartheid movement; apartheid; histories, South African; Indians, South African; politics, South African
South African Indian Congress, protest of Asiatic Land Tenure Act, 31–32
Spivak, Gayatri, 5, 35
Steele, Gwenda Vender, 25n37
struggle, anti-apartheid, 8, 11, 28–29, 38–39, 168–69; literature of, 29, 30, 51
Subbalakshmi, archives of, 14, 24n34
Sulzberger, C.L., 73

Tagore, Rabindranath: *The Home and the World*, 82n23
Tanganyika, Indian plans for, 10, 68
tensions, Afro-Asian, 2; among women, 7; in East Africa, 69, 83n38; intercontinentality of, 8; microeconomics of, 41; in political struggles, 12–13; in South Africa, 41; U.S. understanding of, 6. See also Afro-Asian relationships; solidarity, Afro-Asian
Todorova, Maria, 79, 86n79
Transvaal, satyagraha campaign in, 11
Transvaal Indian Congress, Passive Resistance Council of, 32
treason trialists, South African, 154–56, 162n28, 165n67
Trevor-Roper, Hugh, 80
tribalism, African, 80; caste and, 69–71; democracy in, 83n42

United States: African students in, 116; racial formations of, 5, 6; role in postcolonialism, 15
University of the Witwatersrand, Center for Indian Studies, 8

Vassani, M.G.: *The In-Between World of Vikram Lall*, 17
Verwey, E.J.: *New Dictionary of South African Biography*, 162n28

Verwoerd, Hendrik, 62
Vilakazi, B.W., 55n37

Wilcox, Toni, 150
women: in Cold War politics, 74; in postcolonial development, 114
women, African, 85n64; cross-racial solidarity of, 49; Nyasa, 74; pathologization of, 75; role in anti-imperialism, 74
women, Afro-Asian: tensions among, 7
women, Indian: beauty of, 106, 107, 109, 119n48; contact with Africans, 90, 93, 94–95, 97–107, 109, 113; cross-racial solidarity of, 49; honor of, 11; in Indian developmental projects, 102; mobility of, 35; patriarchal power over, 35–36, 105, 107, 114; resistance to apartheid, 36; sexuality of, 96
women, South African: activism of, 128–32, 134–41, 162n26; cross-racial alliances of, 135
World Cup (Durban, South Africa, 2010), 29, 50
Wright, Richard: *Black Power*, 85n70

Zeenews.com, 8
Zuma, Jacob, 148–50; government of, 150; release from Robben Island, 149
Zuma, Rita, 139

www.ingramcontent.com/pod-product-compliance
Lightning Source LLC
Chambersburg PA
CBHW051541230426
43669CB00015B/2687